English CHALLENGE

GEOFF BARTON

OXFORD
UNIVERSITY PRESS

OXFORD
UNIVERSITY PRESS

Great Clarendon Street, Oxford OX2 6DP

Oxford University Press is a department of the University of Oxford. It furthers the University's objective of excellence in research, scholarship, and education by publishing worldwide in

Oxford New York

Auckland Cape Town Dar es Salaam Hong Kong Karachi Kuala Lumpur Madrid Melbourne Mexico City Nairobi New Delhi Shanghai Taipei Toronto

With offices in

Argentina Austria Brazil Chile Czech Republic France Greece Guatemala Hungary Italy Japan Poland Portugal Singapore South Korea Switzerland Thailand Turkey Ukraine Vietnam

Oxford is a registered trade mark of Oxford University Press in the UK and in certain other countries

© Geoff Barton 2005

The moral rights of the author have been asserted

Database right Oxford University Press (maker)

First published 2005

All rights reserved. No part of this publication may be reproduced, stored in a retrieval system, or transmitted, in any form or by any means, without the prior permission in writing of Oxford University Press, or as expressly permitted by law, or under terms agreed with the appropriate reprographics rights organization. Enquiries concerning reproduction outside the scope of the above should be sent to the Rights Department, Oxford University Press, at the address above

You must not circulate this book in any other binding or cover and you must impose this same condition on any acquirer

British Library Cataloguing in Publication Data

Data available

ISBN-13: 978 0 19 832169 9

10 9 8 7 6 5 4 3 2

Printed by Printplus, China.

Acknowledgments
The Publisher would like to thank the following for permission to reproduce photographs:

p8: Hemera; **p13**: Jamie Harron/Corbis; **p15**: Photodisc/PU; **p18**: Photodisc/OUP; **p21** Movie Store Collection; **p27**: Andrew Grosvenor-Daviees/Rex Features; **p28**: Michael Dalder/Reuters/Corbis; **p36**: Corel/OUP; **p38**: Movie Store Collection; p39: Photodisc/OUP; **p41**: Corel/OUP; **p43**: Corel/OUP; **p44**: Photodisc/OUP; **p46**: Photodisc/OUP; **p48**: Digital Vision/OUP; **p49**: Photodisc/OUP; **p50**: Corel/OUP; **p51**Corel/OUP; **p53**: Ingram Publishing/OUP; **p55**: Corel/OUP; **p56**: Stockbyte/OUP; **p57t**: Stockbyte/OUP; **p57b**: Photodisc; **p61**: Corel/OUP; **p64**: Movie Store Collection; **p67**: Phil Loftus/Capital Pctures; **p70**: Hugh Thompson/Capital Pictures; **p72**: Movie Store Syndication; **p85**: BBC Picture Library; **p86**: Capital Pictures; **p87**: Photodisc/OUP; **p88:** Photodisc/OUP**; p96**: BBC Picture Library; **p101**: Alamy Images; **p103**: Mark Mason/OUP; **p104**: Corbis/OUP; **p107**: Brandon D Cole/Corbis; **p108**: Alamy Images; **p110**; Digital Vision/OUP; **p111**: Digital Vision/OUP; **p113**: Alamy Images; **p114**: Ed Young/Science Photo Lirbrary; **p121**: Ingram Publishing/OUP; **p124**: Hulton-Deutsch Collection/Corbis; **p125**: Jacques M Chenet/Corbis; **p127**: Alamy Images; **p130**: Digital Vision/OUP; **p131**: OUP; **p132**: OUP; **p136**: Illustrated London News/OUP; **p137**: Random House Publishing; **p138:** Bridgeman Art Library; **p139**: Adam Woolfitt/Corbis**; p141**: Photodisc/OUP; **p142**: Hemera; **p143**: Lou Chardonnay/Corbis; **p145t**: Stockbyte/OUP; **p145b**: Corbis/OUP; **p149 both**: Movie Store Collection; **p152**: Bridgeman Art Library; **p157**: Photodisc/OUP; **p159**: OUP; **p163**: Museum of the City of New York/Corbis; **p165**: Apple;

Illustrations are by John Adams: **p 82;** Shirley Bellwood**: p 30;** Bill Greenhead: **pp 35, 97, 146, 151, 167**; Andy Hammond: **pp 20, 59, 65, 101, 147** ; Sarah Horne: **p 94**; Tim Kahane: **pp 63, 99**; Martin McKenna: **p 24**; Oxford Illustrators: **pp 11, 12**; Nicki Palin: **pp 32, 33, 105**; Tom Sperling: **pp 16, 75, 92**; Vincent Vigla: **pp 83, 91, 134, 156.**

Cover image by Jim Zuckerman/Corbis

The author and publisher would like to thank the many teachers, advisers, and schools who assisted in the research and trailing of English Challenge.

We are grateful for permission to reproduce the following copyright material in this book:

Peter Ackroyd: extracts from *Dickens* (Sinclair Stevenson, 1990), reprinted by permission of The Random House Group Ltd. **BBC** news article: 'Children in anti-smacking protest', from BBC news at bbcnews.co.uk, 15 April 2000, reprinted by permission of Article 12 and the BBC. **Peter Baker**: extract from *Making It as a Radio or TV Presenter* (Piatkus Books, 1995), copyright © Peter Baker 1995, reprinted by permission of Watson, Little Ltd. **Hillaire Belloc**: 'Jim' from *Cautionary Verses* (Red Fox, 1995), copyright © Estate of Hilaire Belloc 1930, reprinted by permission of PFD on behalf of the Estate of Hilaire Belloc. **Peter Benchley**: extract from *Jaws* (Deutsch, 1974), reprinted by permission of the Carlton Publishing Group. **Robert Benchley**: 'My Face' from *After 1903 - What?* (Harper & Row, 1938), reprinted by permission of Nathaniel R Benchley. **Alan Bennett**: extract from 'A Chip in the Sugar' from *Talking Heads* (BBC Books, 1990), copyright © Alan Bennett 1988, reprinted by permission of BBC Worldwide Ltd. **Gerard Benson**: parodic poem 'Jack and Jill' from *Imitations of Immortality* edited by E O Parrott (Viking, 1986), reprinted by permission of the author. **Guy Browning**: 'How to use an appliance', *The Guardian*, 29 November 2003, copyright © Guardian Newspapers Ltd 2003, reprinted by permission of Guardian Newspapers Ltd. **Winston Churchill**: extract from 'Blood Sweat and Tears' speech, copyright © Winston S Churchill, reprinted by permission of Curtis Brown Ltd, London on behalf of the Estate of Sir Winston S Churchill. **Arthur C Clarke**: extract from 'The Deep Range' from *The Other Side of the Sky* (V Gollancz Science Fiction, 1961), reprinted by permission of David Higham Associates Ltd. **Kevin Crossley-Holland**: 'The Baker's Daughter' from *British Folk Tales* (Orchard Books, 1987), copyright © Kevin Crossley-Holland 1987, reprinted by permission of the author c/o Rogers, Coleridge & White Ltd, 20 Powis Mews, London W11 1JN. **Crown copyright** material, extract from Home Office Guide to Crime Prevention is reproduced under Class Licence Number C01P0000148 with the permission of the Controller of HMSO and the Queen's Printer. **Richard Curtis** and **Tony Robinson**: extract from *Odysseus: Super Hero* (Hodder Children's Books, 1986), copyright © Richard Curtis and Tony Robinson 1986, reprinted by permission of Berlin Associates. **Kitty Dimbleby**: 'I was smacked but those short, sharp swipes did me good', *Evening Standard*, 7 July 2004, reprinted by permission of the author. **David Hugh Farmer** (ed): extracts 'George and the Dragon' and 'King Canute' from *Oxford Dictionary of Saints* (3e, OUP, 1992), reprinted by permission of Oxford University Press. **Alan Gibbons**: extract from *Shadow of the Minotaur* (Orion Children's Books, 2000), reprinted by permission of the Orion Publishing Group Ltd. **Robert Graves**: 'Warning to Children' from *Complete Poems* (1995), reprinted by permission of the publishers, Carcanet Press Ltd. **Ted Hughes**: 'Ravens' from *Moortown Diary* (1989), reprinted by permission of the publishers, Faber & Faber Ltd. **A J Jacobs** (editor): extracts from *What It Feels Like* (HarperCollins, 2003), reprinted by permission of HarperCollins Publishers Ltd. **Stephen Jones**, Principle, King Edward VI Community College: Letter 'Don't swallow myths about the power of uniform', *Times Educational Supplement*, 30 July 1004, reprinted by permission of the author. **Diane Louise Jordan**: 'My television and Radio Career...' from Sarah Brown (Ed): *Moving On Up* (Ebury Press, 2003), reprinted by permission of the author. **Richard Lewis**: extract from 'Kelly's Dilemma', *Athletics Weekly*, 28 July 2004, reprinted by permission of Descartes Publishing Ltd. **Penelope Lively**: 'Clara's Day' from *Pack of Cards* (Heinemann/Penguin, ***), reprinted by permission of David Higham Associates Ltd. **Sarfraz Manzoor**: 'Anyone can be famous - but the price is high', *The Guardian*, 19 May 2004, copyright © Guardian Newspapers Ltd 2004, reprinted by permission of Guardian Newspapers Ltd. **Rupert Mellor**: 'Star demands: 6 ways to be a travel diva', *The Observer*, 1 August 2004, copyright © Guardian Newspapers Ltd 2004, reprinted by permission of Guardian Newspapers Ltd. **Mike Myers**: extract from screenplay of *Austin Powers: International Man of Mystery* (Pterodactyl Pfilms Ltd), reprinted by permission of Browning, Jacobson & Klein, LLP for the author. **Thomas Nagel**: extract from *What Does it All Mean? A Very Short Introduction to Philosophy* (OUP, 1987), copyright © Thomas Nagel 1987, reprinted by permission of Oxford University Press, Inc. **Joseph O'Connor**: extract from *The Star of the Sea* (Secker & Warburg, 2003), reprinted by permission of The Random House Group Ltd. **Iona and Peter Opie**): 'Goosey, Goosey, Gander' from *Oxford Dictionary of Nursery Rhymes* (OUP, 1951), reprinted by permission of Oxford University Press. **Iona Opie** and **Moira Tatem** (eds): extract from *Oxford Dictionary of Superstitions* (OUP, 1989), reprinted by permission of Oxford University Press. **George Orwell**: extract from *Nineteen Eighty-Four*, copyright © George Orwell 1949, reprinted by permission of A M Heath & Co Ltd on behalf of Bill Hamilton as the Literary Executor of the Estate of the late Sonia Brownell Orwell and of the publishers, Secker and Warburg Ltd. **Dean Pitchford**: extract from the lyrics of 'Fame', words by Dean Pitchford, music by Michael Gore, copyright © EMI Catalogue Partnership, EMI Variety Catalog, Inc, MGM Affiliated Music Inc, and EMI United Partnership Ltd, USA. Worldwide print rights controlled by Warner Bros Publications Inc/IMP Ltd, reprinted by permission of International Music Publishing Ltd. All rights reserved. **Willard Price**: extract from *Amazon Adventure* (Jonathan Cape, 1963), reprinted by permission of The Random House Group Ltd. **Patrick Pringle**: extract from *The Manual of Public Speaking* (Foulsham, 1957), reprinted by permission of W Foulsham & Co Ltd. **Susan Quilliam**: extract from *Body Language* (Carlton Books, 1985), reprinted by permission of the Carlton Publishing Group. **Sophie Radice**: 'Don't mess with me: Britain's rat catchers are losing their fight against the brown rat' from the *Observer Magazine*, 30 November 2003, copyright © Guardian Newspapers Ltd 2003, reprinted by permission of Guardian Newspapers Ltd. **Ronald Reagan**: speech from *Speaking My Mind* (Hutchinson, 1989), reprinted by permission of The Random House Group Ltd. **Eric Schlosser**: extract from *Fast Food Nation* (Allen Lane, 2001), copyright © Eric Schlosser 2001, reprinted by permission of Penguin Books Ltd. **David Sedaris**: extract from *Me Talk Pretty One Day* (Little, Brown & Co, 2000), copyright © David Sedaris 2000, reprinted by permission of Don Congdon Associates, Inc. **Nigel Slater**: extract from *Real Good Food* (Fourth Estate, 1995), copyright © Nigel Slater 1995, reprinted by permission of HarperCollins Publishers Ltd. **Delia Smith**: extract from *How to Cook, Book 1* (BBC Books, 1998), text copyright © Delia Smith 1998, reprinted by permission of BBC Worldwide Ltd. **David Usborne**: 'Shark Practice', *The Independent*, 1 September 2001, copyright © The Independent 2001, reprinted by permission of Independent Newspapers. **Vivienne de Watteville**: extract from *Speak to the Earth: Wanderings and Reflections among Elephants and Mountains* (Methuen, 1940), reprinted by permission of The Random House Group Ltd. **Heathcote Williams**: lines from *Whale Nation* (Jonathan Cape, 1988), reprinted by permission of The Random House Group Ltd.

and also to the following for permission to reproduce the material indicated:

Concept 2 Ltd for 'The Weapon of Mass Reduction', advertisement for indoor rower. **Next plc** for text from packaging 'How to care for and tie your Next tie'. **Python (Monty) Pictures Ltd** for sketch 'The Man Who Speaks in Anagrams' from *Monty Python's Flying Circus*. **The Radio Times** for film review by AJ of *Austin Powers: International Man of Mystery* from www.radiotimes.com. **Supreme Petfoods Ltd** for extract from Reggie Rat leaflet 'How to care for your rat'. **The Times Educational Supplement and the authors** for 'Is Charles Clarke right on uniform? The Education Secretary has launched a war on scruffiness. But is it really such a smart move?', *Times Educational Supplement*, 23 July 2004, YES by Geoff Barton, NO by Kate Petty.

We regret we have been unable to trace and contact all copyright holders of material included before publication. If notified the publisher undertakes to rectify any errors or omissions at the earliest opportunity.

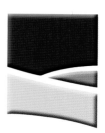

Contents

This book was written for you because you are already showing real promise in English, with the potential to be an exceptional student.

The trouble with books for outstanding students is that they are sometimes dull. They are often packed with dusty old texts that people assume are good for you, but which can be a real chore to get through. It can feel like a punishment for being good at the subject. It's like finishing work early in lessons – only to be given stacks more of the same sort of thing to do. It doesn't encourage you to do your best.

So, the first aim of *English Challenge* is to be lively, entertaining and enjoyable. You'll see from the icons that it combines

 speaking and listening

 reading, and

 writing tasks

– because we know that pace and variety is important in lessons.

There are texts here that you won't find in many English textbooks: for example, an Austin Powers movie script, tales of murders and monsters, updated nursery rhymes, spoofs and parodies, and accounts of people living life 'on the edge'. The aim was to include texts we thought you would enjoy, which would challenge and provoke you, and which would really help you to develop your English skills and knowledge.

STRUCTURE

Here's how the book works:

Each unit starts with a **warm-up**. This is designed to get you thinking, to loosen up your brain. Most of the activities are based on talking or thinking, and they establish the theme for the rest of the unit.

Then there are two or three groups of **texts**. The activities that follow these texts include discussion, exploring language features, and debating your beliefs, which will build your confidence in English. You'll improve your responses to a range of text-types. Stories rub shoulders with poems and non-fiction extracts. You'll become an expert in talking and writing about the main features of a great variety of texts.

Each unit finishes with a choice of **challenges**. These are longer, project-based activities that you can really get your teeth into. They are designed to let you show just how creative, analytical, argumentative or thoughtful you can be, either in writing, or through a talk or debate.

To be successful in anything, you need to know how well you are doing – what your strengths and weaknesses are. The **Assess your learning** section is based on principles of assessment for learning, encouraging you to reflect on how your skills are developing and planning what you need to focus on next. Taken seriously, these sections will help you to build your expertise, step-by-step.

If you finish your work early, then you've made it to the **Finishing line**, a regular section of puzzles, mind-games and challenges. Rather than have to do lots more writing, this section encourages you to think creatively or laterally.

The final unit is a special **test preparation** section. You may not relish the idea of sitting the Key Stage 3 Tests in Year 9, but they do give you an opportunity to show how well you can do under exam conditions. The unit helps you prepare for the tests without simply looking through a lot of past papers. It will help you to identify the exact skills you need to display.

I hope very much that *English Challenge* will enrich your experience of English. I hope it will surprise you, provoke you, and above all, entertain you. It has certainly been great fun to write.

Geoff Barton
Suffolk

Advice bureau

Learning objectives

This unit will develop your ability to:

- Talk and listen confidently in a range of contexts, both formal and informal
- Ask questions to develop ideas that take account of others' views

- Retrieve, collate and summarize information from a range of sources

- Understand and make effective use of paragraphing
- Use a range of sentence structures and varied vocabulary to create effect.

INTRODUCTION

We give and receive advice throughout our lives. It can be in the form of guidance, explanation, persuasive argument, instruction or even poetry. This unit looks at different types of advice, often on the same topic, or in the same form.

WARM-UP

With a partner, test your powers of instruction.

1 Tell your partner how to get from the room you are in to the school reception, BUT … don't move your hands or head. Just use words.

2 Imagine your partner is an alien. He or she has just arrived on Earth and wants to know how to tie a shoelace or a tie. If possible, give him or her a shoelace or tie and explain how to tie it. Again, just use words.

3 From these activities, what have you learnt about the most effective features of instructions?

HOW TO...

The purpose of some advice texts is to help us to do something – such as how to cook a meal, how to put a piece of furniture together, or how to prevent crime.

You might assume that texts like these always have the same style. Texts A, B, and C are three contrasting instructional texts. Read and compare them, thinking in particular about the different styles that the writers use to convey their messages.

6

TEXT (A)

NEXT
HOW TO CARE FOR & TIE YOUR NEXT TIE

With a little care and attention, there is no reason why your Next tie should not afford you many years of wear.

1. Always untie your tie completely after wear. This allows the silk fibres to recover.
2. Always hang your tie when not in use. This will allow any heavy creases to drop out naturally.

All Next ties are dry cleanable, although please ensure you choose a reputable company.

Four-In-Hand

1. Cross long end over short end. 2. Bring long end under short end. 3. Bring long end over front. 4. Bring long end up through neck-band. 5. Bring long end down through knot. 6. Complete the knot.

1   2   3   4   5   6

Half-Windsor

1. The tie's wide end should be over a foot below the narrow end. Cross it over the narrow end and bring it back underneath. 2. Take up the wide end and wind it once through the loop from front to back. 3. Now pass the wide end of the tie across the front of the knot and bring it through the loop again before passing it down through the front of the knot. Finally, slowly tighten the knot as you draw it up to the collar. 4. Slide the completed knot in place.

1   2   3   4

TEXT B

HOW TO...
USE AN APPLIANCE
GUY BROWNING

THERE ARE A NUMBER of labour-saving appliances in the kitchen that do things you wouldn't do anyway. Foremost of these is the breadmaker, followed by the yogurt-maker and the juicer. These save labour by virtue of the fact that no one uses them.

When people buy a breadmaker, they think it's the best thing since sliced bread, but soon realise that, when you feel like a quick sandwich, the last thing you want to do is drag sacks of grain in from the shed.

Appliances are called labour-saving because, once you have one, you don't have to do any work. People who have a washing machine, say, no longer have to do any washing – all you have to do is sort the wash, load the machine, put powder in the machine, program the machine, empty the machine and hang out the washing . . .

A washing machine is like a child in reverse. It starts with dirty clothes, plays for an hour or two by itself, then has clean clothes. It also demands to be fed twice a day and keeps you awake at night when it gets overexcited. Washing machines, like mobile phones, used to be newfangled. Now, everyone has one, but for some reason washing machines have not got smaller, like mobile phones.

The shower is a self-loading appliance where you put yourself in, select the wash cycle and then give yourself a good scrub. Some people's cycles go on for as long as an average dishwasher. One can only assume they have a lot of baked-in dirt . . .

Our reliance on the appliance is almost total, which is why many of us go for the extended warranty with a 24-hour on-site service. This costs the same as having a new appliance every year, but it's worth it to know you'll always be able to make yogurt at 3am.

From the *Guardian Weekend*, 29 November 2003

Personal safety

■ After dark, park in a well-lit, busy place. Look around before you get out. If you're parking in daylight, but coming back for your car at night, think about how things will look in the dark.

■ Have your key ready when you go back to your car. Make sure there is no-one in the car.

■ If your car develops problems, find a telephone. On motorways follow the marker arrows to the closest phone. They are never placed any more than a mile apart, on opposite sides of the motorway. These phones accurately pinpoint your location so that an emergency vehicle can speedily assist you. **Never** cross the carriageway to use a phone.

■ While on the hard shoulder or telephoning, keep a sharp look-out and don't accept lifts from strangers – wait for the police or breakdown service. Don't stay in the car, but wait on the embankment nearby with the front passenger door open. If someone approaches you or you feel threatened, lock yourself in the car and speak to them through a small gap in the window.

■ Remaining in your stationary vehicle can be extremely hazardous. Only if you have a disability which prevents your leaving it, should you remain within the vehicle and switch on your hazard warning light to summon help from a passing police patrol car. An in-car phone would assist you to summon help in an emergency but you must know your exact position.

What men can do

Men can help by taking the issue of women's safety seriously in their everyday lives. Bear these points in mind:

■ If you are walking in the same direction as a woman on her own, don't walk behind her – this may worry her. Cross the road and walk on the other side. This may reassure her that you are not following her.

■ Don't sit too close to a woman on her own in a railway carriage or bus.

■ Realise how threatening actions such as staring, whistling, passing comments and jostling can be, particularly when you are one of a group of men.

Unintentional intimidation - can men help women feel safer?

From *Your Practical Guide to Crime Prevention*, Home Office, 7 January 2001

ACTIVITIES

1 Work in pairs or a small group. Read the statements in the grid below and refer to Texts A, B and C. Rank the texts according to the statements.

If you disagree about the order, try to justify your own opinion. For example, 'I think Text B is the most humorous because of the way it describes …'

Statements	Rank order of texts
a) The most informative text is …	
b) The easiest text to understand is …	
c) The most humorous text is …	
d) The text with the most personal tone is …	
e) The text that has the most appropriate style for its purpose is …	

2 Look closely at Text A again. Then sketch out a similar instructional text for making tea or cleaning your teeth, using a mix of words and diagrams.

3 Text B takes a light-hearted view of the subject.
  a) Note three humorous features in the article.
  b) Imagine that the article is a serious text about 'How to use an appliance'. The language is likely to be different from Guy Browning's:
    ✦ it might use the second-person voice (e.g. 'You should start by …')
    ✦ it might use imperative verbs at the beginning of sentences (e.g. 'Open the door')
    ✦ it might use some technical vocabulary.
  c) Write the opening paragraphs of a serious text about how to use an appliance, such as a DVD or a washing machine. Annotate (label) your text showing the instructional features you have used (e.g. the sentence types, vocabulary choice).

4 Refer back to Text C.
  a) Which do you think are the three most important pieces of advice?
  b) How does the writer try to make the tone reassuring?
  c) Sketch out plans for converting this text into an A4 poster aimed at school students of your own age.
    ✦ Which pieces of advice from the text would you use?
    ✦ How would you re-present them?

RATING RATS

 Different texts can present different perceptions of their subject. Look closely at the following examples. Text D is part of a leaflet giving advice on caring for your pet rat (and is also advertising pet-care products). Text E is part of a magazine article about the horrors of the brown rat.

As you read the extracts, think about the way the writers use language to shape our responses to rats – the first making us sympathetic to them; the second making our flesh creep.

TEXT D

Caring for your RAT

Hi. I'm Reggie Rat...

No, don't be scared – like all fancy rats, I'm very friendly. Not to mention very smart and affectionate, and playful!

If you've got a pet rat, then read on to find out how to give him the kind of life he deserves...

Unlike some other rodents, we're diurnal, which means we're awake and ready to play during the day. We're very social animals and get lonely and unhappy if kept alone. We're very easy to look after, so it's best to get a pair.

Two boys or two girls will live happily together if they are littermates. A boy and girl rat will get on together, but they'll also have babies!

Did you know?
Fancy rats are completely different to wild rats. Don't be taken in by all you read and hear – we really make wonderful pets and delightful companions.

Housing

We like lots of space in which to run around, play and climb, so get a big, tall cage to keep your rat happy. A solid floor will avoid foot injuries.

Avoid wooden cages which your rat will chew through! Converted aquariums or aviaries make good homes for rats. It's best to house rats indoors, in an outhouse or shed if not in the house.

Position the cage somewhere light and airy, off the floor and away from draughts, heaters, direct sunlight, petrol fumes and other pets. Never put the cage on or near a fridge, television, radio or hi-fi.

Provide plenty of warm bedding, like my favourite – Russel Bedding – which is really soft and fluffy.

Feeding time!

It's best to feed your rat at the same time each day around late afternoon. We'll soon settle quite happily into a routine and will get excited when we hear the sounds we associate with feeding time.

Always make sure your rat has access to fresh, clean drinking water, which should be changed every day.

How much to feed your rat:
The average rat will eat around 15–17gms of Reggie Rat each day (that's about 3 teaspoons!)

Rat basics

We also love ladders, perches and swings. Exercise wheels are best avoided as we can damage our feet and tails in the spokes, and most of them are too small anyway.

We're athletic too, so let your rat out of the cage to have a run around the room, but close doors and windows first and never leave him unsupervised. Also, cover electric wires, because we love to chew!

In addition to a cage, food and toys, you'll need a water bottle and food bowl. Provide your rat with an enclosed box in his cage, so he can have some privacy.

Exercise
We're very acrobatic and need plenty of exercise. Climbing's one of our favourite activities so why not give your rat some nice tall branches to clamber up and down?

Reggie's checklist

- Clean and refill the water bottle
- Empty the food bowl and refill with Reggie Rat food
- Remove any soiled bedding and replace with Russel Bedding
- Check your rat for any signs of ill health
- Check the length of your rat's teeth and nails – consult your vet if they're too long
- Spend time with your rat – isn't that why you wanted him in the first place?

Don't mess with me

Britain's rat-catchers are losing their fight against the brown rat.

Sophie Radice

It was midnight and I was asleep, which is why I didn't leap out of bed when I heard my husband cry out from the bathroom, next door. By the time I had roused myself he was standing by the airing cupboard in his boxers, with his trousers around his ankles and a heavy piece of wood in his hand.

He stopped me coming closer by air-spelling 'R-A-T'. I ran back to bed with my heart thumping. My alarm increased when, about half an hour later, he gave up trying to hit it on the head and joined me.

'It was bigger than any rat I ever saw on my travels in India,' he said, shocked. 'I was on the loo and it came slowly towards me. I got up and fell over because my trousers were round my ankles, and that's when it ran past me and into the airing cupboard.' Neither of us slept much that night . . .

We called the council the next morning. The pest control officer (he didn't want to be called a rat-catcher) told us that we couldn't lay poison down because we had a dog. He said that the hot summer and warm autumn were ideal breeding conditions for the brown rat (aka Norway rat). The increase in smelly litter because of the heat had, in his opinion, enticed the rats out of the sewers. He had been told by the council that there had been a 56 per cent increase in the rat population in the past five years, and that there

Rats pose a greater problem in rural areas, as pest control is more prevalent in towns and cities.

were now six million rats in the UK.

He also told us some revolting facts: that rats urinate 80 times and defecate 40 times each day, and even though most of us associate rats with the plague (the fleas jumped from dead rats to humans, who passed on the infection) it is Weil's disease – which has flu-like symptoms but can go on to damage the liver – that we should be more concerned about these days. This is usually spread through rat's urine. He said rats could spread diseases to people in multiple ways: through the lice or disease-carrying fleas that live on rats, through their droppings and urine and even by biting people . . .

Dr Joanne Webster, reader in parasitical epidemiology at Oxford University, has studied both rural and urban populations of rats. 'What was really interesting was that when we

compared the rural rats with urban rats, we found fewer parasites on the city rats, which is perhaps contrary to what people might expect. This is because there are denser populations of rats in the country than in the city, where there is greater pest control . . .

My husband was taking no chances. Using peanut butter as bait on great big traps and working out where the rat runs were – using flour, so that he could see their footprints – he killed seven in the first wave. He would shout up the stairs in triumph each morning. It took him four months to get the king rat, and when he did he seemed slightly flat, as if life had suddenly lost part of its meaning . . .

Rat Facts

1 Rats eat rubbish, leftover dog food, bird food and even dog excrement.
2 Rats can crawl through holes as small as a 10 pence piece.
3 Rats are amazing survivors: they can land unharmed after a five-storey fall, jump three feet in the air and tread water for three days.
4 Rats are the only wild animal the SAS are banned from eating while out in the field, because of health implications.

From the *Observer* Magazine, 30 November 2003

ACTIVITIES

1 Complete a grid to compare the ways in which the writers of Texts D and E make us feel positive or negative towards rats.

Text D – positive	Text E – negative
The writer often uses the first person, to make the rat sound chatty and friendly	

2 a) Choose one sentence from each text that you think best sums up the writer's attitude to the subject.

b) Compare your choice of sentences with someone else's and discuss why you chose them. In your discussion:
  ✦ ask questions of your partner to draw out her or his ideas
  ✦ show how carefully you are listening to these ideas, by asking questions that explore them further – such as, 'So which word in particular do you think conveys …?/ Why do you think that image makes the reader feel …?'

3 Imagine you have a pet rat called Tufty. You think rats have a bad image and, in your view, are cute and adorable. Write a short letter or email to the writer of Text E, Sophie Radice, saying why you think she needs to take a more open-minded approach to rats.
  ✦ Say that you think writers in the media have a responsibility to present a balanced case.
  ✦ Describe the reasons you find Tufty such an amiable pet.

4 Here are six quotations about keeping pets. Some are serious; most are humorous. Working with a partner, discuss which ones you like most and least.

I

If a dog jumps in your lap, it is because he is fond of you; but if a cat does the same thing, it is because your lap is warmer.
Alfred North Whitehead (1861–1947)

II

We call them dumb animals, and so they are, for they cannot tell us how they feel, but they do not suffer less because they have no words.
Anna Sewell (1820–1878), *Black Beauty*, 1877

III

I loathe people who keep dogs. They are cowards who haven't got the guts to bite people themselves.

August Strindberg (1849–1912), *A Madman's Diary*, 1895

IV

Cats are smarter than dogs. You can't get eight cats to pull a sled through snow.

Joe Weinstein

V

A boy can learn a lot from a dog: obedience, loyalty, and the importance of turning around three times before lying down.

Robert Benchley (1889–1945)

VI

I like pigs. Dogs look up to us. Cats look down on us. Pigs treat us as equals.

Sir Winston Churchill (1874–1965)

5 Read this opinion:

'Keeping pets is a really outdated idea. It's how humans try to show they are in control by making animals rely upon them for food, shelter and affection. The latest fashion for exotic pets, such as rats, spiders and snakes is even worse. The owners are just desperate attention-seekers who need to grow up.'

Work in two teams to put together the arguments for and against the idea of keeping pets.

+ Organize your ideas into three to five main points.
+ Work with a partner to present your case.
+ End with a vote from the rest of the class to show which team they think has won the argument.

ADULTS KNOW BEST

We can easily assume that advice texts take the form of articles and instructions. In fact, poetry has often been used to 'instruct'. In the eighteenth and nineteenth centuries this kind of poetry was especially popular, helping to reinforce a clear sense of right and wrong.

Read the following three poems. They are all written by adults and aimed at young people. Each poem gives advice – sometimes seriously, sometimes tongue-in-cheek. As you read, think about the similarities and differences between the poems.

Jim

by Hilaire Belloc

There was a Boy whose name was Jim;
His Friends were very good to him.
They gave him Tea, and Cakes, and Jam,
And slices of delicious Ham,
And Chocolate with pink inside
And little Tricycles to ride,
And read him Stories through and through,
And even took him to the Zoo –
But there it was the dreadful Fate
Befell him, which I now relate.

You know – or at least you ought to know,
For I have often told you so –
That Children never are allowed
To leave their Nurses in a Crowd;
Now this was Jim's especial Foible,
He ran away when he was able,
And on this inauspicious day
He slipped his hand and ran away!
He hadn't gone a yard when – Bang!
With open Jaws, a lion sprang,
And hungrily began to eat
The Boy: beginning at his feet.

Now, just imagine how it feels
When first your toes and then your heels,
And then by gradual degrees,
Your shins and ankles, calves and knees,
Are slowly eaten, bit by bit
No wonder Jim detested it!
No wonder that he shouted 'Hi!'

The Honest Keeper heard his cry,
Though very fat he almost ran
To help the little gentleman.
'Ponto!' he ordered as he came
(For Ponto was the Lion's name),
'Ponto!' he cried, with angry Frown,
'Let go, Sir! Down, Sir! Put it down!'

The Lion made a sudden stop,
He let the Dainty Morsel drop,
And slunk reluctant to his Cage,
Snarling with Disappointed Rage.
But when he bent him over Jim,
The Honest Keeper's Eyes were dim.
The Lion having reached his Head,
The Miserable Boy was dead!
When Nurse informed his Parents, they
Were more Concerned than I can say: –
His Mother, as She dried her eyes,
Said, 'Well – it gives me no surprise,
He would not do as he was told!'
His Father, who was self-controlled,
Bade all the children round attend
To James's miserable end,
And always keep a-hold of Nurse
For fear of finding something worse.

TEXT G

Warning to Children
by Robert Graves

Children, if you dare to think
Of the greatness, rareness, muchness,
Fewness of this precious only
Endless world in which you say
You live, you think of things like this:
Blocks of slate enclosing dappled
Red and green, enclosing tawny
Yellow nets, enclosing white
And black acres of dominoes,
Where a neat brown paper parcel
Tempts you to untie the string.
In the parcel a small island,
On the island a large tree,
On the tree a husky fruit.
Strip the husk and pare the rind off:
In the kernel you will see
Blocks of slate enclosed by dappled

Red and green, enclosed by tawny
Yellow nets, enclosed by white
And black acres of dominoes,
Where the same brown paper parcel –
Children, leave the string untied!
For who dares undo the parcel
Finds himself at once inside it,
On the island, in the fruit,
Blocks of slate about his head,
Finds himself enclosed by dappled
Green and red, enclosed by yellow
Tawny nets, enclosed by black
And white acres of dominoes,
With the same brown paper parcel
Still untied upon his knee.
And, if he then should dare to think
Of the fewness, muchness, rareness,
Greatness of this endless only
Precious world in which he says
He lives – he then unties the string.

ACTIVITIES

1 Each poem offers some advice. Compare the two poems using these statement-starters:
   ✦ The main advice or message in Text F/G is …
   ✦ The most humorous poem is …
   ✦ The most serious poem is …
   ✦ The historical order in which the poems were probably written is …

2 Look more closely at Text G.
   a) As a piece of advice to children, what do you think it is saying?
   b) Discuss the ideas that interest or confuse you.
   c) Consider the writer's use of language. Explore its main message.
   d) Why do you think Robert Graves presented his ideas in a poem?
   e) What other text type might the subject lend itself to?
   f) Write a paragraph using the questions above to describe your personal response to the poem, saying finally what you like or dislike about it.

UNIT CHALLENGES

1. Investigation

Choose a topic you are knowledgeable about – such as a hobby, place or event of special interest. Investigate a number of different texts on this subject – such as leaflets, instructions, websites, books.

a) Put together an advice sheet (approximately one side of an A4 sheet) to guide people on materials which will help them learn about this topic. Advise your reader on the best sources of information and warn them away from the worst!
    You might base this on the consumer reports produced in *Which?* magazine and on their website (www.which.net) or similar sites (www.consumerreports.org).

b) Decide on the best system for presenting your findings, e.g. star ratings, graphs, short paragraphs of text, quotations.

c) Call your study something like 'The Expert Guide to xxxx xxxx'.

2. Storytelling

Think more about stories and poems that are designed to give advice.

a) Look at some more comic examples, such as Roald Dahl's *Revolting Rhymes*, Hilaire Belloc's *Cautionary Tales* or Stanley Holloway's monologue 'Stanley and the Lion'. All of them use verse to tell an entertaining tale with a moral purpose.

b) Write your own advice poem addressed to adults. Choose a theme such as 'How to be a good parent' or 'How to avoid embarrassing your children'.

Think carefully about how you will convey your advice – perhaps by making your main character a parent and showing how her or his actions lead to trouble.

3. Opinion piece

Based on your debate about keeping pets, write an article of about 500–700 words for a newspaper. Give your opinion on:

a) keeping pets

b) why pets are especially important for some people (e.g. companionship for the elderly)

c) exotic pets such as tarantulas and snakes.

✦ Look at the way newspaper and magazine columnists write opinion pieces – often weekly articles on an issue they feel strongly about. You might look at the work of Melanie Phillips who writes in the *Daily Mail* or Julie Burchill who writes in the *Times*.

✦ Remember that, as a journalist, you need to catch your reader's interest from the start, so think of something attention grabbing – an anecdote, fact or statistic.

✦ Unlike essays, newspaper and magazine articles tend to use short paragraphs – often with just two sentences per paragraph. This keeps the reader's eye moving down the page and adds a sense of pace.

✦ Build your argument in short paragraphs, making your piece as lively and controversial as possible.

ASSESS YOUR LEARNING

Look back at the learning objectives for this unit:

● Talk and listen confidently in a range of contexts, both formal and informal
● Ask questions to develop ideas that take account of others' views

Make brief notes on the following:
a) How well did you work in paired and small groups? Which are you more comfortable in?
b) How can you demonstrate that your listening skills are improving?
c) How have you used questions to draw out someone else's views?
d) What would be a good activity to help you to develop your speaking and listening?

● Retrieve, collate and summarize information from a range of sources

This unit has given you various opportunities to read texts, compare them, choose key ideas and summarize them.
a) Which of these reading skills do you think you are developing most effectively?
b) Give yourself a rating *, ** or *** for each of these reading skills:
    ✦ reading texts quickly
    ✦ absorbing key ideas
    ✦ being able to find important parts of a text
    ✦ spotting similarities and differences between texts
    ✦ commenting on writers' use of language.

Use this to think about how you might practise your main area for reading development.

● Understand and make effective use of paragraphing
● Use a range of sentence structures and varied vocabulary to create effect

Look back and think carefully about how you have practised these skills.

a) In which text types might you expect to use very short paragraphs? Why? In which would longer paragraphs be more appropriate? Why?
b) Put these texts in rank order depending on whether you would generally expect to use simple or complex sentences and vocabulary:

Most simple ⟶ most complex

✦ An article on a specialist topic written for a specialist audience
✦ A newspaper story in a tabloid newspaper (e.g. the Sun)
✦ A story for children under five years old
✦ An instruction leaflet for installing a DVD player
✦ An opinion piece about vegetarianism in a magazine

THE FINISHING LINE

Look at the cartoon below. Imagine that it is part of an advice text. Think of five captions that could accompany this cartoon. Make your ideas as wacky as possible!

Heroes and villains

Learning objectives

This unit will develop your ability to:

- Give a talk that engages your listener through varied expression and vocabulary
- Pay close attention to other people's views
- Use standard English fluently in a formal situation

- Identify key features, themes and characters, and relevant information to support your views
- Give a personal response to literary texts, referring to language, structure and themes

- Write, engaging and holding the reader's interest, showing a variety of styles, including a formal style where appropriate
- Use imaginative and precise vocabulary
- Understand and experiment with paragraphing.

INTRODUCTION

Throughout history, people have felt the need to have heroes and heroines to act as role models, and villains to hate and fear. Some heroes and villains have survived through centuries, and their names are known to millions. Others are making their reputations today. This unit looks at the portrayal of heroes and villains, real and imaginary, in poems, stories, magazine articles and autobiographies.

WARM-UP

1 In the film, *Spider-Man 2*, May Parker addresses her grandson, Peter. She talks about the young boy across the street who hero-worships Spider-Man.

HE KNOWS A HERO WHEN HE SEES ONE. TOO FEW CHARACTERS OUT THERE, FLYING AROUND LIKE THAT, SAVING OLD GIRLS LIKE ME. AND LORD KNOWS, KIDS LIKE HENRY NEED A HERO. COURAGEOUS, SELF-SACRIFICING PEOPLE. SETTING EXAMPLES FOR ALL OF US. EVERYBODY LOVES A HERO. PEOPLE LINE UP FOR THEM, CHEER THEM, SCREAM THEIR NAMES. AND YEARS LATER, THEY'LL TELL HOW THEY STOOD IN THE RAIN FOR HOURS JUST TO GET A GLIMPSE OF THE ONE WHO TAUGHT THEM HOW TO HOLD ON A SECOND LONGER. I BELIEVE THERE'S A HERO IN ALL OF US, THAT KEEPS US HONEST, GIVES US STRENGTH, MAKES US NOBLE, AND FINALLY ALLOWS US TO DIE WITH PRIDE, EVEN THOUGH SOMETIMES WE HAVE TO BE STEADY, AND GIVE UP THE THING WE WANT THE MOST. EVEN OUR DREAMS.

With a partner, or in a group, discuss these questions:
- ✦ Why do we need heroes and heroines?
- ✦ Can you think of real people in the world of music, films or TV who are regarded as role models?
- ✦ Is it unfashionable to admire someone?
- ✦ Who would your hero or heroine be? (Think of someone who you think sets a good example with their personal qualities, outlook and lifestyle.)

2 Many stories are about the fight between good and evil. Make a list of ten stories or films that are based on a single hero or heroine, who fights against dark, evil forces.

Harry Potter
Tomb Raider
(Lara Croft)

HEROES AND RIVALS

Texts A and B both focus on heroes, but the authors use very different styles to describe them. In *Odysseus: Super Hero* (Text A), Tony Robinson and Richard Curtis retell the classic Greek tale first told in the *Iliad*, an epic poem written by Homer in 800 BC. As you read it, notice how the authors update the story for a modern audience.

In *Shadow of the Minotaur* by Alan Gibbons (Text B), a boy uses a powerful computer game to transform into the Greek hero, Theseus. As you read it, think carefully about the writer's style and the mood it conveys.

The entire Greek army had been sitting on the wet grass for hours listening to Archbishop Calchas' sermon.

'And now,' droned the Archbishop, 'for the final part of our funeral service.'

Diomedes stifled a yawn and clouted the soldier in front of him, who was playing patience with a pack of cards.

'Our old hero Achilles is dead,' continued Calchas. 'We cannot win the war until we have a new hero.'

General Agamemnon now stepped forward in his best uniform and lifted up the huge suit of silver and gold armour.

'This belonged to my dearest friend, Achilles,' he said with tears in his eyes. 'I now present it to the best and bravest soldier in the Greek army: he shall be our new hero.'

The soldiers stirred. At last the moment had arrived. Who would it be? Which man among them was great enough to take over from Achilles?

Big Ajax stood up. 'Thank you very much.' He said. 'It's a great honour.'

'Sit down!' shouted Diomedes.

'What do you mean?' answered Ajax. 'I'm the best soldier in the Greek army. I've got sacks full of medals to prove it.'

'Rubbish!' shouted Diomedes.

'Oh, rubbish is it? Who do you think's the best then? Your marvellous friend, Odysseus, I suppose.'

'YES!' roared Odysseus' men.

'NO!' roared Ajax's men, and they began jostling and shoving each other and someone was biting someone else's nose.

'Stop it! Stop it! Stop it!' yelled Agamemnon, wading in and pulling them apart. 'This is a church service, not a football match. We'll have a vote. All those in favour of Odysseus being our hero, raise your swords.'

A forest of swords rose into the air.

'Right, swords down. All those in favour of Ajax.'

Another forest of swords appeared.

'Who's the winner then?' asked the Archbishop, unable to disguise the excitement in his voice. 'Is it Ajax or is it Odysseus?'

'It's a draw,' said Agamemnon.

'Well, then, let's ask the Trojans what they think,' called Diomedes. 'After all, the best hero is the one the enemy is most scared of.'

So that evening, Agamemnon and Calchas crept up to the walls of Troy and listened carefully to the guards moving above them on the battlements.

'I don't fancy our chances now Hector's dead,' they heard a Trojan say.

'No,' replied someone else. 'I certainly wouldn't want to meet that Ajax on a dark night.'

'Ajax? You great nellie! It's Odysseus you want to worry about. He may be little but he's as crafty as a barrelful of monkeys.'

'Yes,' they all agreed. 'If anyone can win the war for the Greeks, it's Odysseus.'

So that night there was a big banquet and Odysseus was presented with the armour. There were long, boring speeches of course, but they were all followed by roast ox, swan pie and gallons of wine, and soon the entire army was merry — except for Ajax, who was sitting in the corner. The merrier the army got, the gloomier Ajax became.

Odysseus went over to him and said, 'It's not important. It's a fuss about nothing. The armour's too big for me any way.'

Ajax turned white. 'To be humiliated is bad enough,' he said. 'But to be humiliated by a smarmy, pint-sized know-it-all like you is more than I can bear. Leave me alone! I'm going to kill myself!'

And he ripped open his shirt, drew his sword, and fell on it. Except his sword bent double under his weight and he collapsed on the floor.

The whole Greek army burst out laughing. 'Leave him alone,' scoffed Diomedes. 'He'll soon get over it.'

'I hope so,' replied Odysseus, and stared hard at the bowed figure of Ajax.

TEXT B

The first of the beast's roars almost tore the flesh from his bones. The second, a nerve-splitting bellow that crushed inside his brain, very nearly made him give in before he'd even begun his challenge. He glanced back at the hatch in the door through which he'd just walked and saw the reassuring smile of the dark-eyed girl on the other side. Mustering his own thin smile, he knelt down and picked up the things he'd dropped, a sword with a finely-wrought handle and a ball of strong, thick string.

'You can do this,' he told himself. 'You really can do this.'

But he hadn't convinced his body he could do it. His first attempt at tying the string to the door failed. He was so nervous his fingers just wouldn't work. It was like wearing mittens and trying to knot raw sausages. Taking a deep, shuddering breath he finally managed to pass the string through the hatch and secure it to one of the little bars in the opening. Weighing the sword uncertainly in his hand and letting the string play out behind him, he took his first faltering steps down the dark passageway. The blackness clung to him, trying to crawl inside his skin. The maze of tunnels was everything he'd been expecting – and more. They had the mystery of night, the terror of loneliness. They lay deep beneath the earth, where the sun never shone and the fresh wind never blew, and the silence there was heavy. The air was clogged with a choking animal musk. The walls of the tunnel by the entrance were smooth and regular, built from huge blocks of stone. But as he penetrated deeper into the gloom, he noticed a change. The walls were worn and they were slippery with something thick and slimy. Blood maybe. He flinched then walked on, his feet thudding dully in the cold, still air. Those echoing footsteps shook the close, uncomfortable blackness that clutched at him like a hand. No more than fifty paces from the door the tunnel branched in half a dozen different directions.

He moved forward, unrolling the ball of thread as he went, and stopped. He was still considering his options when he heard the beast again. This time the sound was a low, throaty growl. It was closer, and moving purposefully towards him.

'It's stalking me.'

In the darkness he stumbled and reached out to steady himself. The moment his hand came into contact with the cold stone surface, he recoiled in horror. It was blood all right. There was no mistaking its greasy slide. The walls were slippery with the stuff. The stone floor too. That wasn't all; there were splintered bones, matted hair, gobbets of torn flesh. The tunnels were a slaughterhouse.

'Ugh!'

He immediately wished he hadn't given in so readily to his feeling of disgust. His voice resounded loudly through the tunnels, inviting the beast to attack.

'Now it knows,' he murmured. 'It knows where I am.'

As if to confirm the fact, the beast bellowed through the passageways, mad with rage and hunger. This time the noise was so loud and so shattering that everything around him seemed on the verge of coming apart. The dust began to fall in fine spirals from the ceiling. It was out there in the darkness, snorting and panting, preparing to charge.

'What are you waiting for? Why don't you just do it?'

His breath was coming in troubled gasps. He gripped the sword tightly and edged forward. That's when he noticed a change in the lighting of the tunnel. A shaft of hazy light slanted onto him from above. He looked up and saw a face gazing down at him, the sympathetic face of the girl who had handed him the sword and the ball of string.

'The beast is coming,' she said.

'I know.'

ACTIVITIES

1 Look back at Text A. What kind of hero is Odysseus? Use a spider diagram to note his different qualities.

2 Classic tales are sometimes retold in a formal style – like this:

> During the Trojan war Odysseus played an important part. Together with Diomedes he stole king Rhesus' horses, but the very next day he was wounded in battle. When Achilles was killed, a new leader was required. There were long and detailed discussions about who would best serve the role of leader – Odysseus or Ajax. Because of his reputation as a fearsome warrior, Odysseus was chosen, leaving Ajax feeling alienated and humiliated. Although Odysseus tried to show friendship, Ajax's bitterness was too strong, and the two men parted for ever.

Tony Robinson uses a more informal style. Write down five features of style that make his text informal and bring it alive. You might consider:

- characterization
- description
- story structure and paragraphing
- use of language – such as word choice.

3 In Text B, Alan Gibbons holds the reader's attention by using emotive language – words that create an emotional impact. For example, 'nerve-splitting', 'terror' and 'loneliness' all convey very intense feelings. Gibbons also uses metaphors and similes to make the scene vivid. For example, 'It was like wearing mittens and trying to knot raw sausages.'

Working with a partner, choose three more examples of the writer's interesting use of language. Explain why you think each example works well.

4 Test how clearly the writer portrays the scene by sketching it, working from the description in the text. Label the key features of the scene.

5 With a partner, or in a small group, discuss the following questions:
- Which of the two texts do you prefer and why?
- Is it really possible to express a preference because they are so different?
- Are the two texts aimed at different types of readers? Explain your thinking.

GOOD AND BAD INFLUENCES

This section explores the importance of role models. It contains three text types – an autobiographical essay, a magazine article and a biographical extract. In the first piece, Diane Louise Jordan talks about the positive influences people have on her life. In the second, Kelly Holmes is portrayed as a role model for sportswomen. The third extract tells the story of a Victorian doctor who was secretly a murderer – a 'role model' who was not what he seemed.

TEXT C

Diane Louise Jordan

TV and Radio Presenter and Motivational Speaker

My television and radio career began back in January 1990 when I became the first black presenter on *Blue Peter*. I am currently a regular face on *Songs of Praise*. However, over the last 12 years I have presented such a variety of programmes that I've been described as 'a presenter across boundaries'! I also work closely with a number of charities, all of which reflect issues close to my heart. I am a Vice President of NCH and Patron of many other organisations. I was asked to sit on the *Diana, Princess of Wales Memorial Committee*, and am also very proud to be one of the trustees for the BBC's long-running and hugely successful *Children In Need Appeal*. My underlying passion to encourage, motivate and inspire all people to be the best they can possibly be, coupled with the many requests to speak at corporate and charity events, inspired me to launch my corporate speaking company, *Chronicle21*.

My career in the media can be traced back to a schoolmate's challenge to apply for drama school. At the time I was hugely self-conscious and uncomfortable with the thought of even reading out loud in class! So the prospect of a career reliant on speaking publicly was near anathema to me! However, always being one to rise to a challenge, my acceptance eventually resulted in constant work as a professional actress for seven years before joining *Blue Peter*.

For me, relationship is the key to success, both in life and work. There have been some remarkable relationships in my life that have had and continue to have a significant impact on me. My 16-year-old daughter inspires me – when I'm getting flustered about work this relationship reminds me what my true priorities are. I have also always known the unconditional love of my parents – their utter belief in me as a person, regardless of merit, has underpinned my sense of self-worth. My late grandfather was a very wise man whose steady principles and strong values are imprinted on my heart. For example, my determination to do my best and 'see things through' is a principle based on these wise words imparted from him – 'No matter what you do, whether you're running the country or cleaning it, always do it with at least 100 per cent of your ability.'

There's a saying that 'behind every successful and fulfilled person is an inspiring teacher'. My inspiring teacher is Mrs Morton who believed in me when I didn't even believe in myself. She was tough, exacting and fearsome. She expected high results from her pupils, and worked with and encouraged us to achieve them – which with her kind of support, we did.

My Advice: *I am so often asked, 'How do I become a television presenter?' If I am honest, I really don't have a simple answer. However, I do believe that becoming a 'success' at anything involves beginning to know and accept who you are. Start with the inside out! I've learned that the most important thing in life is to VALUE yourself. We all have an intrinsic 'worth' – something special about us, something valuable to offer – to make a difference to the world. Approach all you do with integrity and tenacity; have the courage to live your dreams.*

TEXT D

Kelly's dilemma

by Richard Lewis

… By the time of the Olympic Games in Beijing in 2008, Kelly Holmes expects to be retired but we cannot bank on that because one of the finest servants in British athletics history has a habit of delivering the unexpected.

But, she said, the Olympics in Athens, which open in two weeks' time, will be her last appearance at such an event and she does not want to leave Greece, or let alone wake up with a startling realisation in years to come that she wished she had achieved more.

It is why she will spend the next fortnight deciding whether to run the 800m or the 1500m in Athens, or both …

Holmes is the Olympic bronze medallist and world silver medallist at the 800m which should mean there is no argument. But such has been her constant desire to become a champion at 1500m at one of the Worlds, it is not quite as straight-forward as that.

The Norwich Union International, a match between Britain, USA, the Commonwealth and Europe, at the Alexander Stadium on Sunday, was her first appearance since she had revealed that she is suffering psychologically from not finding her rhythm or her race conviction in the 1500m this season.

It goes back to the world indoor final in Budapest in March, when she fell before finishing ninth. "I am going into races now aware of what other people are doing when normally I just concentrate on myself," she said.

But if she has been worried about being in doubt over the way she runs 1500m, what do we make of the 800m? Watching Holmes run in Birmingham, you could hardly imagine that this was an athlete with any sort of problem.

She played it steady over the opening lap, settling on the outside of the pack that included fellow Britons Hayley Tullett and Susan Scott, and Jennifer Toomey of the USA.

Jolanda Ceplak, the European champion and the fastest woman in the world this year with her time of 1:57.68, was the barrier that Holmes was going to have set herself against and when the Slovenian moved to the front, the reaction of the Briton was important.

Doubting the way she runs? Not on this performance. She bided her time and as the tempo increased along the back straight, Holmes, 34, took off.

She moved from fifth to first in a blink of an eyelid and she was gone. Her arms were pumping full throttle, by the bend she was ahead and by the time she had moved into the final 80m, her lead was growing all the time.

As she crossed the line, after her winning position was never challenged, she flung her arms around in the air to celebrate one of the best wins of her season. She had trimphed in 2:00.46 from Ceplak (2:01.75) and Tullett (2:02.32).

But the race was Holmes at her very best, having not trained much in the previous week after a re-occurrence of a calf problem that had troubled her last year.

She has such overriding emotional strength that any time she has suffered an injury, from the pain and the tears that come with it, she somehow finds the resilience to bounce back. Otherwise, she would have quit a long time ago.

But still she cannot decide what the best move will be for Athens and which event will be the best to run.

She competes in the 1500m at today's Norwich Union London Grand Prix at Crystal Palace and the outcome of that could go some of the way to making her decision. Yet with Maria Mutola, her training partner, failing to make an impression this season because of her slow return to form following a hamstring injury, Holmes would arguably be a clear medal favourite – even a genuine gold medal contender – for the 800m because of the experience, success and power she has over the distance.

If Mutola was missing from the 800m, Ceplak and Russian Olga Kotlyarova, who has season's best of 1:57.96, would remain major threats but Holmes, with a 2004 best of 1:58.71, might be best to opt for this distance because Turkey's Sureyya Ayhan remains so dominant in the 1500m.

Holmes is entered into both the middle-distance events in Athens. The timetable means it would be a monumental performance to achieve something in both because there is no break between the final of the 800m before the heats of the 1500m the next day, but she said "I still have time to make a decision and this is what I am going to do.

"I just wanted to run out there today. I felt comfortable and thought if I am going to go, just go and whatever I have got, it will come out.

"It didn't matter who was in the field, it was a tough competition anyway. I just needed that race for myself and I just have to start believing in myself and home in on what I want.

"You do need a lot of confidence in this game and I have always said that most of your performance comes from 80 per cent of what you believe in …"

Doctor Webster

Murder at Harvard

Until the gray and melancholy twenty-third of November, people of Boston, like most Americans, had been talking all through 1849 of nothing but the great California gold rush. But on that Friday, Boston had something nearer home to occupy its attention. Dr. George Parkman had disappeared in broad daylight. It was as incredible as if Bunker Hill Monument had sunk into the bowls of the earth. A Boston Parkman simply did not, could not, disappear and leave no trace. The police went to work, and so did hundreds of citizens, spurred by a reward of $3000 for the doctor, alive or dead.

That day the eminent doctor had left his Beacon Hill home about noon. He had gone to the Merchants' Bank. From there he had called at a greengrocer's to leave an order. Later he had been seen walking rapidly toward Harvard Medical College. At or near the college, it appeared, he had walked straight into Valhalla …

Professor John White Webster made a call on the missing man's brother, and said that he had had an interview with the doctor in the Medical College on Friday afternoon, at which time he had paid Dr. Parkman $483. Dr. Parkman had then left the college, said the professor.

Webster, a graduate of Harvard Medical, had taught chemistry at Harvard for more than twenty years. With their four pretty daughters, the Websters were noted for the hospitality they lavished on the faculty. His professor's salary of $1200 annually was wholly inadequate. While it was known that Webster owed the doctor money and that the doctor had gone to collect it, the professor was not under suspicion. Who could suspect a faculty member of Harvard? It began to look as if some thug had waylaid the doctor, done away with him and made off with the $483 which Webster said he had paid Parkman.

Apparently nobody suspected Webster – except a morose and obscure man named Ephraim Littlefield, a janitor at Harvard Medical College. It appears to have been a generous act of Webster's that set Littlefield on his trail like a hound of hell. On the Tuesday following Parkman's disappearance, Webster presented a thumping big turkey to Littlefield – the first gift the janitor had received in seven years of work at the college. Littlefield not only brooded over the gift, but he was troubled because talk on the street had it that 'they'll sure find Dr. Parkman's body somewhere in the Medical College.' Medical colleges in those days were held to be notorious receivers of the products of professional body snatchers.

'I got tired,' said Littlefield in explaining his next move, 'of all that talk.' Accordingly, into his dismal basement apartment at the college he lugged drills, hammers, chisels, crowbars. He told his startled wife that he was going to dig through the brick vault under Professor Webster's laboratory room. Mrs. Littlefield was dreadfully frightened; suspicion of a Harvard professor was an act against nature, perhaps even against God.

A few days before Parkman's disappearance, the janitor explained to her, he was helping Webster in his laboratory. Suddenly Dr. Parkman appeared before them, 'Dr. Webster,' he cried, 'are you ready for me tonight?' Webster replied: 'No, I am not ready tonight.' Parkman shook his cane. 'Dr. Webster,' he said savagely, 'something must be accomplished tomorrow.' Then he left.

For the next several days, Littlefield had brooded and wondered whether on the next call Professor Webster *had* been ready. 'And *now*,' said the janitor to his wife, 'what do you think?'

So on Thanksgiving Day, while the turkey sputtered in the oven, he hammered and drilled his way into the solid brick wall. Progress was slow, but Littlefield was as determined as he was suspicious. At noon he refreshed himself with the great bird and cranberries, then returned to his labors. He continued his work on Friday, after his regular duties, and that night broke through. 'I held my light forward,' he related, 'and the first thing I saw was the pelvis of a man and two parts of a leg. I knew,' he added darkly, 'this was no place for such things.'

Littlefield called the police. Within a short time Webster was in a cell of the city jail. Next day the press and the town went delirious. 'Horrible Suspicions!!' screamed the normally sedate *Transcript*. 'Arrest of Professor J. W. Webster!' Harvard College and Beacon Hill seemed about to tumble into the Charles River.

Professor Webster was put on trial on the nineteenth of March, 1850. The state's star witness, janitor Littlefield, took the stand and his testimony was bad indeed for the professor. The defence presented a long and distinguished array of character and other witnesses. President Sparks of Harvard thought Webster 'kind and humane.' Nathaniel Bowditch, son of the celebrated mathematician, believed Webster to be 'irritable though kind-hearted.' Oliver Wendell Holmes testified both for the defence and the state. For the latter, he said that whoever had cut up the body alleged to be that of Dr. Parkman had certainly been handy with surgical knives.

The state was attempting to prove that the remnants of human mortality discovered in the vault – and in the laboratory stove – were those of Dr. Parkman; and the defence was doing its best to prove the fragments to have been almost anybody but Dr. Parkman. Day after day the trial continued and much of Boston sought to get into the courtroom. The marshal

cleared the visitors' gallery every ten minutes, thus permitting thousands of persons to witness portions of the event of the century.

Slowly the coils closed around Professor Webster; and late on the eleventh day the jury was charged by Chief Justice Lemuel Shaw in an address which is still considered by lawyers to be one of the great expositions of all time on the subject of circumstantial evidence. Three hours later the jury returned a verdict of guilty.

Long before Professor Webster was hanged on August 30 1850, he made a confession. On that fatal Friday, Parkman had called Webster a scoundrel and furiously shaken his cane in the Professor's face. Then, said Webster, 'I felt nothing but the sting of his words, and in my fury I seized a stick of wood and dealt him a blow with all the force that passion could give it.' One blow was enough. Parkman fell, bleeding at the mouth. Webster bolted the doors, stripped the dead man, hoisted him into the sink and then dismembered him with the deft professional strokes that had been admired by Dr. Holmes.

The painful celebrity that came to Harvard has been dissipated in the century that has intervened, but more than one member of the faculty long felt the blight cast by Professor Webster. Bliss Perry once related how his mother, at Williamstown, Massachusetts, refused to entertain a Harvard professor who had come there, some twenty years after the crime, as a delegate to a convention of New England college officials. Mrs. Perry vowed firmly that she could not sleep 'if one of those Harvard professors was in the house.'

ACTIVITIES

1 In Text C, Diane Jordan mentions three people who have had and still have a profound influence on her life. Who are they? Summarize how they have influenced her.

2 In pairs, interview one another about a member of your family or a teacher who has a positive influence upon you.

Interviewer:
Ask structured, open-ended questions that encourage your guest to develop points, rather than answer in single words. For example:
+ Who was the person who most influenced you and how?
+ What is your earliest memory of this person?
+ Tell me more about what she/he looked like.
+ What in particular do you remember about her/him?
Respond to your guest's comments rather than stick to a planned set of questions. If she/he says something that you would like to hear more about, ask for further details.

Interviewee:
Try to give full answers. Describe the person, bringing her/him to life for your interviewer by including humorous or interesting details. Focus on how they looked, sounded, and what effect they had on you, and others.

3 What are the main facts that we learn about Kelly Holmes from Text D? Note them on a spider diagram.

4 How does Richard Lewis, writer of Text D, imply that Kelly Holmes is a good role model?

5 Text D was written for a magazine called *Weekly Athletics*, which is aimed at readers with a special interest in the topic. What clues in the text indicate it was written for a specialist rather than general audience?

6 Look back at Text E. Doctor Webster was someone most people respected and trusted but who proved to be a villain. Design a graph that charts his fall from hero to villain.
+ On the X axis, plot the main events or revelations that led to a change in people's perceptions of Doctor Webster.
+ On the Y axis, chart the high and low points of his career.

7 Villainous doctors have fascinated people throughout recent history. Imagine a tabloid newspaper reporting the case of Doctor Webster today.

a) Write a headline for the story.

b) Write the first two paragraphs of the news story.

Remember:

+ A tabloid headline is rarely longer than five words. It often misses out grammatical words such as 'the' and 'their'.

+ The first sentence of a newspaper article is usually a topic sentence – it should tell the reader something about who, what, where and when.

+ Paragraphs in a tabloid newspaper are usually just one or two sentences long.

ENCOUNTER WITH A DRAGON

This section looks at two texts. They both recount the legend of the hero, Saint George, and his encounter with the dragon. Text F is an account from *The Oxford Dictionary of Saints*. As you read it, notice how much information is packed into the short text.

Text G is from a very long poem called 'The Faerie Queene' written by Edmund Spenser. It was published in 1596, around the time that Shakespeare was establishing himself as a major playwright. As you read it, remember that it was written more than 300 years ago, so some of the language needs careful thought. You may find it helpful to read it aloud, or with a partner, so you can share ideas about untangling the more difficult parts.

TEXT F

THE DRAGON, a local pest which terrorised the whole country, poisoned with its breath all who approached it. Every day it was appeased with an offering of two sheep, but when these grew scarce, a human victim, chosen by lot, was to be substituted instead. The lot had fallen on the king's daughter, who went to her fate dressed as a bride. But George attacked the dragon, piercing it with his lance, and led it captive with the princess's girdle [belt], as if it were completely tame. George told the people not to be afraid: if they would believe in Jesus Christ and be baptised he would rid them of this monster. The king and people agreed; George killed the dragon and 15,000 were baptised. George would take no reward, but asked the king to maintain churches, honour priests, and show compassion to the poor.

from *The Oxford Dictionary of Saints, edited by David Hugh Farmer*

FROM 'THE FAERIE QUEENE', BOOK I, CANTO XI

by Edmund Spenser

The Knight of the Red Cross meets the dragon.

By this, the dreadful Beast drew nigh to hand,
Halfe flying and halfe footing in his haste,
That with his largenesse measured much land,
And made wide shadow under his huge waste,
As mountaine doth the valley overcaste.
Approaching nigh, he reared high afore,
His body monstrous, horrible, and vaste;
Which, to increase his wondrous greatnes more,
Was swoln with wrath and poyson, and with bloody gore;

And over all with brasen scales was armd,
Like plated cote of steele, so couched neare
That nought mote perce; ne might his corse bee harmd
With dint of swerd, nor push of pointed speare:
Which as an Eagle, seeing pray appeare,
His aery plumes doth rouze, full rudely dight;
So shaked he, that horror was to heare:
For as the clashing of an Armor bright,
Such noyse his rouzed scales did send unto the knight.

His flaggy winges, when forth he did display,
Were like two sayles, in which the hollow wynd
Is gathered full, and worketh speedy way:
And eke the pennes, that did his pineons bynd,
Were like mayne-yardes with flying canvas lynd;
With which whenas him list the ayre to beat,
And there by force unwonted passage fynd,
The cloudes before him fledd for terror great,
And all the hevens stood still amazed with his threat.

His huge long tayle, wownd up in hundred foldes,
Does overspred his long bras-scaly back,
Whose wreathed boughtes when ever he unfoldes,
And thick entangled knots adown does slack,
Bespotted as with shields of red and blacke,
It sweepeth all the land behind him farre,
And of three furlongs does but litle lacke,
And at the point two stinges in fixed arre,
Both deadly sharp, that sharpest steele exceeden farre.

But stinges and sharpest steele did far exceed
The sharpnesse of his cruel rending clawes:
Dead was it sure, as sure as death in deed,
What ever thing does touch his ravenous pawes,
Or what within his reach he ever drawes.
But his most hideous head my tongue to tell
Does tremble; for his deepe devouring jawes
Wyde gaped, like the griesly mouth of hell,
Through which into his darke abysse all ravin fell.

And, that more wondrous was, in either jaw
Three ranckes of yron teeth enraunged were,
In which yett trickling blood, and gobbets raw,
Of late devoured bodies did appeare,
That sight thereof bredd cold congealed feare;
Which to increase, and all atonce to kill,
A cloud of smoothering smoke, and sulphure seare,
Out of his stinking gorge forth steemed still,
That all the ayre about with smoke and stench did fill.

ACTIVITIES

I Compare Texts F and G, thinking about the following features:
   a) the amount of action
   b) the amount of description
   c) the purpose of the texts
   d) the impact on the reader.

Write your answers in a grid.

Features	The Oxford Dictionary of Saints	The Faerie Queene
Action		
Description		
Purpose		
Impact		

2 Think about your experience of reading the poem (Text G). Answer the following questions, with your partner if you read in pairs.
   a) On a scale of 1 to 5, how difficult or easy was it to understand? (1 = very hard)
   b) Choose three features of Spenser's language that you found particularly interesting, vivid or challenging. Give examples and explain your reaction to them.
   c) Were there any parts of the text that you found impossible to untangle? What research might help you to understand it?

3 In Text G we learn a lot about the dragon (the villain of the tale), but not much about George (the hero). Using the clues in the poem, draw a quick sketch of the dragon in Spenser's poem. Use quotations from the poem to label the details of its appearance.

UNIT CHALLENGES

1. Writing the opening of a heroic tale

Take the storyline of George and the Dragon and write the opening of a modern version. Revise the story as 'Georgina and the Dragon' if you wish. Choose one of two styles:

either

✦ a light-hearted version, like Tony Robinson and Richard Curtis created for the Odysseus myth

or

✦ a dark and sinister version, using a style similar to the one that Alan Gibbon uses.

HINTS ON STYLE

✦ Focus on the quality rather than the quantity. Don't tell the story too quickly, but use description and dialogue to reveal details of setting and character.

✦ Choose your narrative voice: first person (e.g. 'Many people had warned me to expect a creature of extraordinary ugliness, but nothing had prepared me for the sight, or stench, of what I encountered …'); or third person (e.g. 'As George edged closer to the great olive tree, he felt a rumbling of the ground through his feet and up his legs …').

✦ Consider using a split narrative: an opening paragraph describing the dragon; then cut to a paragraph of the villagers in terror, or George preparing for battle.

✦ Create a powerful impact through your choice of words: lots of sensuous words (sight, sound, touch, etc.) and active verbs (avoiding is/was/has), and a variety of simple and complex sentences.

2. Villains in a debate

Organize a balloon debate with a group of five to eight people. One of the class could play chairperson, introducing each villain, summing up the arguments, and supervising the voting process. Follow steps a to f, below:

a) Each person takes on the role of a villain of their choice. The villain might be a historical person, a politician or a fictional character from a book or film.

b) Imagine that this group of villains are together in a hot-air balloon sailing high in the sky. But the balloon is in trouble and loses height. One person needs to be sacrificed (thrown out of the balloon) for the others to survive. Who should it be?

c) Each 'character' prepares a three-minute speech, explaining why he or she should remain in the balloon.

d) Each character delivers his or her speech.
e) After the speeches, members of the audience (group) discuss who to eject and who to keep. They should comment on the delivery of the speeches (volume, fluency, etc.) as well as the actual content (strength of arguments, entertainment value, etc.).
f) The audience vote on who to eject from the balloon.

During the debate, use standard English, which is the formal style of English used in the media and in most written texts. So, avoid regional dialect and slang expressions – stick to words that you would find in a dictionary.

3. Personal writing

Refer back to Dianne Jordan's essay about the influences on her life, then decide who has had a major influence on your own life. Choose two or three of these people and write an account of them in a short essay entitled 'Positive Influences'. These people might be teachers, members of your family, friends or even celebrities whom you admire.

For each person you choose, say something about:
✦ who the person is
✦ her looks/personality/values
✦ your memory of her/him
✦ an influential event or incident that you remember well
✦ what it is about this person that especially inspires you.

In your writing try to avoid using 'I' and 'me' too much, which could make it feel repetitive. Aim for a more detached style by focusing on the people you are describing, like this:

'Roy Samson was a powerful early influence. His teaching style was unusual and sometimes very eccentric. One day ...'

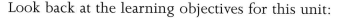

ASSESS YOUR LEARNING

Look back at the learning objectives for this unit:

- Give a talk that engages your listener through varied expression and vocabulary
- Pay close attention to other people's views
- Use standard English fluently in a formal situation

a) Think about your performance in the balloon debate and the feedback from the audience.

b) Give yourself a rating * to ***** on each of these aspects:
  - ✦ volume
  - ✦ fluency
  - ✦ strength of arguments
  - ✦ attention to others' speeches
  - ✦ entertainment value.

c) Note down an idea for how you could improve on your weakest aspect.

d) If you were asked 'What is standard English?' could you give a full explanation? Write down one sentence in standard English as an example, and one sentence in non-standard English.

- Identify key features, themes and characters, and relevant information to support your views
- Give a personal response to literary texts, referring to language, structure and themes

Think of the range of literary texts you have read in this unit: *Odysseus*, *Shadow of the Minotaur*, and *George and the Dragon*.

a) How well can you sum up the key points about characters, themes and language? (You might want to jot them down.)

b) One feature of very high quality literature work is being able to justify your viewpoint by referring to the language of the text. Can you back-up your key points with evidence from the text?

- Write, engaging and holding the reader's interest, showing a variety of styles, including a formal style where appropriate
- Use imaginative and precise vocabulary
- Further improve your understanding of paragraphing

a) Draw a half-page panel and label it 'Best Bits'.

b) Skim the creative or personal writing you have done in this unit. Pick out three examples of words, sentences, or a language decision (e.g. using first rather than third person voice, organization of material into paragraphs) which show the way you have developed your writing.

THE FINISHING LINE

Here are five anagrams. They are all famous heroes or villains. How quickly can you work them out?

CRUEL HES
SAD MEN RIP
MAN AT COW
HARD ADVERT
ATTIRE NORM

Learning objectives

By the end of this unit you should be able to:

- Adapt your talk to different contexts with increasing confidence
- Take an active part in discussion, showing understanding of ideas and sensitivity

- Identify different layers of meaning and comment on their significance and effect
- Summarize a range of information from different sources

- Adapt your style and register to different forms, including an impersonal style
- Write in a neat, legible form
- Use a range of punctuation to clarify meaning

INTRODUCTION

This unit is about extreme experiences, such as travelling through hostile environments, suffering shark attacks, plane crashes, avalanches, and facing the powerful forces of nature. The texts are from autobiographical accounts, stories and poems, and they all convey what it is like to experience life 'on the edge'.

(**WARM UP**)

I To survive this unit you will need excellent thinking skills. Test yourself here. If **none** of the following statements are true, who can we assume broke the window?

Rob: Sara broke the window.
Paul: Rob will tell you who broke the window.
Kate: Paul, Rob and I could not have broken the window.
Alex: I did not break the window.
Oscar: Rob broke the window, so Paul and Kate couldn't have.
James: I broke the window, so Paul is innocent.

2 Some people love extreme sports, such as bungee jumping, skiing in remote mountains, skydiving. Other people say:

'It's a very reckless kind of hobby. These people don't just put themselves at risk; they also risk the lives of the emergency services who may end up having to sort out the problems when things go wrong. Personally, I wouldn't allow amateurs to do any extreme sports.'

What do you think? What are the arguments for and against?

3 Consider the following five sound bites about challenge, risk and adventure.

a) What do you understand by each one?

b) Which do you most agree with?

c) Which do you like best?

I

Challenge is a dragon with a gift in its mouth …Tame the dragon and the gift is yours.

Noela Evans

II

I don't think you can measure life in terms of years. I think longevity doesn't necessarily have anything to do with happiness. I mean happiness comes from facing challenges and going out on a limb and taking risks. If you're not willing to take a risk for something you really care about, you might as well be dead.

Diane Frolov and Andrew Schneider

III

Nobody is ever met at the airport when beginning a new adventure. It's just not done.

Elizabeth Warnock Fernea

IV

Life is either a daring adventure or nothing. Security does not exist in nature, nor do the children of mankind as a whole experience it. Avoiding danger is no safer in the long run than exposure.

Helen Keller

V

It is only in adventure that some people succeed in knowing themselves – in finding themselves.

André Gide

TRAVEL DETECTIVES

Nowadays, cheap airline flights have made overseas travel very popular and millions of people go abroad for long and short breaks. However, travelling in the past was more difficult, more expensive and often more dangerous. Fewer people travelled, but their written accounts were very popular.

This section looks at five accounts of exotic travel. They are presented without details of who wrote them, when they were written, or whether they are fact or fiction. That's your challenge: to find out which text is which. There is a grid on page 47 to fill in your answers. Here are some clues about the texts:

✦ Two of them are fiction; four are non-fiction.
✦ They were written at different times: 1690, 1796, 1884, 1911, 1902, 1963.
✦ One was written for children.
✦ Two were written by women; four by men.

TEXT Ⓐ

Going up that river was like travelling back to the earliest beginnings of the world, when vegetation rioted on the earth and the big trees were kings. An empty stream, a great silence, an impenetrable forest. The air was warm, thick, heavy, sluggish. There was no joy in the brilliance of sunshine. The long stretches of the waterway ran on, deserted, into the gloom of overshadowed distances. On silvery sandbanks hippos and alligators sunned themselves side by side. The broadening waters flowed through a mob of wooded islands; you lost your way on that river as you would in a desert, and butted all day long against shoals, trying to find the channel, till you thought yourself bewitched and cut off for ever from everything you had known once – somewhere – far away – in another existence perhaps. There were moments when one's past came back to one, as it will sometimes when you have not a moment to spare to yourself; but it came in the shape of an unrestful and noisy dream, remembered with wonder amongst the overwhelming realities of this strange world of plants, and water, and silence. And this stillness of life did not in the least resemble a peace. It was the stillness of an implacable force brooding over an inscrutable intention. It looked at you with a vengeful aspect. I got used to it afterwards; I did not see it any more; I had no time. I had to keep guessing at the channel; I had to discern, mostly by inspiration, the signs of hidden banks; I watched for sunken stones; I was learning to clap my teeth smartly before my heart flew out, when I shaved by a fluke some infernal sly old snag that would have ripped the life out of the tin-pot steamboat and drowned all the pilgrims; I had to keep a look-out for the signs of dead wood we could cut up in the night for the next day's steaming. When you have to attend to things of that sort, to the mere incidents of the surface, the reality – the reality, I tell you – fades.

We marched yesterday thirteen and a half hours without getting anywhere. We set off at five in a delicious still night with a temperature of 36 – it felt quite balmy. The sun rose clear and beautiful as we passed through the gates of our valley into a wide low plain – we were to reach the Wady Hauran, which is the father of all valleys in this desert, in ten hours, and the little ruin of Muheiwir in half an hour more and there was to be plentiful clear water. We were in good spirits, as you might imagine; the Sheikh sang songs of Nejd and Ali instructed me in all the desert roads. We rode on and on. At two o'clock I asked Ali whether it were two hours to Muheiwir? "More," said he. "Three?" said I. "Oh, lady, more." "Four?" I asked with a little sinking of heart. "Wallahi, not so much." We rode on over low hills and hollow plains. At five we dropped into the second of the valleys el Ud. By this time Fattuh and I were on ahead and Ali was anxiously scanning the landscape from every high rock. The Sheikh had sat down to smoke a narghileh while the baggage camels came up. "My lady," said Fattuh, "I do not think we shall reach water to-night." And the whole supply of water which we had was about a cupful in my flask. We went on for another half-hour down the valley and finally, in concert with Ali, selected a spot for a camp. It was waterless, but, said he, the water was not more than two hours off: he would take skins and fetch some, and meantime the starving camels would eat trees. But when the others came up, the Father of Camels, Abdullah, he from whom we hired our beasts, protested that he must have water to mix the camel meal that night (they eat a kind of dough), and rather against our better judgement we went on. We rode an hour farther, by which time it was pitch dark. Then Muhiyyed Din came up to me and said that if by chance we were to meet a ghazu in the dark night it might go ill with us. That there was reason in this was admitted by all; we dumped down where we stood, in spite of the darkness Fattuh had my tent up before you could wink, while I hobbled my mare and hunted among the camel loads for my bed. No one else put up a tent; they drew the camels together and under the shelter they gave made a fire of what trees they could find. Fattuh and I divided the water in my flask into two parts; with half we made some tea which he and I shared over some tinned meat and some bread; the other half we kept for the next morning when I shared it with the sheikh. We were none of us thirsty really; this weather does not make you thirsty. But my poor little mare had not drunk for two days, and she whinnied to everyone she saw. The last thing I heard before I went to sleep was the good Fattuh reasoning with her. "There is no water," he was saying. "There is none. Ma fi, ma fi."

I had got within six yards, and yet I remained unnoticed, the head of the buffalo being turned slightly from me, and I not making much noise. I was not destined to go much further. A step or two more and there was a rustling among some dead leaves. Simultaneously the buffalo's head turned in my direction. A ferocious, blood-curdling grunt instantly apprised me of the brute's resolution to be revenged. The next moment it was on its feet. Unprepared to fire, and completely taken by surprise, I had no time for thought. Instinctively I turned my back upon my infuriated enemy. As far as my recollections serve me, I had no feeling of fear while I was running away. I am almost confident that I was not putting my best foot foremost, and that I felt as if the whole affair was rather a well-played game. It was a game, however, that did not last long. I was aware of Brahim tearing away in front of me. There was a loud crashing behind me. Then something touched me on the thigh, and I was promptly propelled skyward.

My next recollection was finding myself lying dazed and bruised, with some hazy notion that I had better take care! With this indefinite sense of something unusual I slowly and painfully raised my head, and lo! there was the brutal avenger standing three yards off, watching his victim, but apparently disdaining to hoist an inert foe. I found I was lying with my head towards the buffalo. Strangely enough even then, though I was in what may be called the jaws of death, I had not the slightest sensation of dread; only the electric thought flashed through my brain, 'If he comes for me

again I am a dead man.' It almost seemed to me as if my thought roused the buffalo to action. Seeing signs of life in my hitherto inanimate body, he blew a terrible blast through his nostrils, and prepared to finish me off. Stunned and bruised as I was, I could make no fight for life. I simply dropped my head down among the grass in the vague hope that it might escape being pounded into jelly. Just at that moment a rifle-shot rang through the forest, which caused me to raise my head once more. With glad surprise I found the buffalo's tail presented to my delighted contemplation. Instinctively seizing the unexpected moment of grace, I with a terrible effort pulled myself together and staggered away a few steps. As I did so, I happened to put my hand down to my thigh, and there I felt something warm and wet; exploring further, my fingers found their way into a big hole in my thigh. As I made this discovery there was quite a volley, and I saw my adversary drop dead …

TEXT D

Hal had never met anybody quite like the colonel. The man was harmless enough, so long as he only wanted his picture taken. But a fool was a dangerous person to have along on a safari. This fake Hunter would have to be watched. He might get himself and everybody else into serious trouble.

A scream behind him made him turn round. The colonel was already in trouble. He was dancing and prancing, yelling at the top of his voice, ripping off his jacket, shirt and trousers, slapping his body and stamping his feet.

Hal could guess what had happened. He had seen soldier ants at work during his Amazon journey. Now the ants had been attracted by the leopard's carcass, and when the colonel placed his foot on the animal's head the ants had swarmed up his legs and were puncturing every part of his body with red-hot needles.

Hal ran back into camp. He did not run fast enough to suit the colonel.

'Hurry up! I'm being eaten alive. Do you want 'em to kill me?'

He was astounded when Hal paid no attention to him. Hal had something else to think of besides a dancing colonel.

Soldier ants are one of the greatest terrors of the tropical jungle. They march across the country like an army and devour everything in their path. They swarm over their prey in a thick blanket. They can strip the hide from an elephant.

'Make fire!' he yelled to the Africans. 'A ring of fire all round the camp.'

The ants already in the camp were bad enough. But behind them would be a column of soldiers perhaps a mile long, marching steadily towards the camp.

The colonel would have to take care of himself.

Hal dashed into his father's tent. If the ants attacked a helpless man he might be killed.

'Ants!' Hal cried.

His father needed only that one word to get the whole story.

'None here, Hal. The hippo. Quick!'

Hal was out again and racing to the hippo's cage. He would open the cage and let the animal escape rather than allow it to be murdered by the ravenous ants. The hippo was trembling with fear, for even the largest animals know this danger and dread it. But the ants had not yet climbed the wheels of the truck. Hal jumped into the driver's seat, started the engine, and drove the truck several hundred yards out of camp.

His next thought was for the baby leopards and the dog. He came running back to the camp site, whacking as he ran the few ants that had managed to get on his body.

He found the dog and the spotted kittens huddled together, while Joro thrashed the ground around them with an old shirt, driving away the ants.

To Hal, this was an amazing sight. Here was truly a man divided against himself. Joro was pledged to be a murderer. He was ready to kill men. The savage was strong and fierce within him – yet also inside him was a very gentle heart that prompted him to protect two leopard cubs and a dog.

His own body was not free of the biting ants, but he let them bite as he beat away the danger from the whimpering animals.

44

The canoes of these inland sailors are truly primitive craft: they are hollowed out of the trunks of single trees by means of iron adzes; and, if the tree has a bend, so has the canoe. I liked the frank and manly bearing of these men, and, instead of sitting in the waggon, preferred a seat in one of the canoes. I found they regarded their rude vessels as an Arab does his camel. They have always fires in them, and prefer sleeping in them while on a journey to spending the night on shore. "On land you have lions" – say they – "serpents, hyaenas, and your enemies; but in your canoe, behind a bank of reed, nothing can harm you." Their submissive disposition leads to their villages being frequently visited by hungry strangers. We had a pot on the fire in the canoe by the way, and when we drew near the villages devoured the contents. When fully satisfied ourselves I found we could all look upon any intruders with perfect complacency, and show the pot in proof of having devoured the last morsel.

While ascending in this way the beautifully wooded river we came to a large stream flowing into it. This was the river Tamunak'le. I inquired whence it came. "Oh, from the country full of rivers – so many no one can tell their number – and full of large trees!" This was the first confirmation of statements I had heard from the Bakwains who had been with Sebituane, that the country beyond was not "the large sandy plateau" of the philosophers. The prospect of a highway capable of being traversed by boats to an entirely unexplored and very populous region, grew from that time forward stronger and stronger in my mind; so much so, that, when we actually came to the lake, this idea occupied such a large portion of my mental vision that the actual discovery seemed of but little importance.

Twelve days after our departure from the waggons at Ngabisane we came to the north-east end of Lake Ngami; and on the 1st of August, 1849, we went down together to the broad part, and, for the first time, this fine-looking sheet of water was beheld by Europeans.

I was taken by the *Indians* when *Casco* Fort was taken. My Husband being slain, and four Children taken with me. The Eldest of my Sons they kill'd, about two Months after I was taken, and the rest scatter'd from me. I was now left a Widow, and as bereav'd of my Children; though I had them alive, yet it was very seldom that I could see 'em ... We had no Corn or Bread; but sometimes *Groundnuts, Acorns, Purslain, Hogweed,* Weeds, Roots and sometimes *Dogs Flesh,* but not sufficient to satisfie Hunger with these; having but little at a time. We had no Success at hunting save that one Bear was killed, which I had part of; and a very small part of a Turtle I had another time, and once an *Indian* gave me a piece of a *Moose's* Liver, which was a sweet Morsel to me; and *Fish* if we could catch it. Thus I continued with them, hurry'd up and down the Wilderness, from May 20, till the middle of *February*; carrying continually a great Burden in our Travels; and I must go their Pace, or else be killed presently; and yet was pinch'd with Cold for want of Cloathing, being put by them into an *Indian* Dress, with a sleight Blanket, no Stockins, and but one pair of *Indian* Shooes, and of their Leather Stockins for the Winter: My Feet were pricked with sharp Stones and prickly Bushes sometimes, and other times pinch'd with Snow, Cold, and Ice, that I travell'd upon, ready to be frozen, and faint for want of Food; so that many times I thought I could go no further, but must lie down, and if they would kill me, let 'em kill me. Yet then the Lord did so renew my Strength, that I went on still further as my Master would have me, and held out with them. Though many English were taken, and I was brought to some of 'em at times, while we were about *Casco Bay* and *Kennebeck River*, yet at *Norridgawock* we were separated, and no *English* were in our Company, but one *John York* and myself, who were both almost starv'd for Want; and yet told, that if we could not hold up to travel with them, they would kill us. And accordingly *John York* growing weak by his Wants, they killed him, and threatened me with the like.

ACTIVITIES

1 Working on your own or with a partner, copy and complete this grid to record what you can work out about each text. Give the main clue that has helped you reach each conclusion.

Text	Fiction or non-fiction?	Written for adults or children?	Male or female writer?	Location (can you tell which continent or country?)	Date of text?
A					
B					
C					
D					
E					
F					

2 Think about the key ingredients in good travel writing.

a) Look at the list below and put the ingredients in rank order.
   - Set in an exotic location
   - Describing a dangerous situation
   - Insight into the people who live there
   - Description of travel arrangements
   - Description of unusual customs and habits of local people
   - Description of wild plants and creatures
   - Imaginative, vivid language (powerful vocabulary, similes, metaphors, etc.)
   - An interesting narrator

b) Are there any points that you think should NOT be included in the list?

3 Write a paragraph or two about the travel extracts you like best. Explain the reasons for your choice.

EXTREME SITUATIONS

The following texts look at how people cope in times of crisis. Text G contains extracts of people's accounts of what it was like to face extreme danger. Text H is a newspaper article by a journalist who went on a shark safari. Text I is an extract from Peter Benchley's famous novel, *Jaws*.

As you read the three texts, think about the ways the writers describe the different experiences. For example, do the writers seem fascinated, detached, or horrified?

TEXT G

...TO BE iN A PLANE CRASH

Ellen Hassman, 55, retired advertising executive

Trays were in the upright position, and all hand luggage was stored for landing. Being a nervous flyer to begin with, I remember feeling great relief when I heard the wheels touch the runway. Then it happened. The plane began to increase in speed. I knew something was wrong. I can still feel the blood drain from my face. The plane shook and rattled, trying to lift into the air again. People began to scream. The plane veered to the left and my body was thrown against the window. I looked at the ground as it reached up for us, and I knew we were going to crash. My life didn't flash in front of my eyes. I shook, I cried and I cursed. A stream of swearwords came from my mouth. I was angry. I didn't want to feel pain. I wanted to live, and I wanted to die quickly. I cried for my life that would never be. I didn't cry for those I would leave behind. Why should I? They would still be alive. My tears were solely for me and the 'why me?' of it. I remember being angry at those who were screaming, because their screams were disturbing my precious last moments.

And then I heard nothing but the sound of wrenching metal as the body of the plane met the ground, first class first. I closed by eyes, and the sound of metal twisting and tearing ripped through my head. I covered my ears with my hands, trying to stop the assault, and then we began to slide. We slid for ever, like a car out of control on ice.

I opened my eyes to the sun shining on my face. There was nothing in front of me. The body of the plane had broken away at my feet. The stewardess and I were the only ones in the detached section of the plane's tail. In front of us, we could see the rest of the plane and the passengers continuing to slide as they headed towards disaster and eventual explosion. I jumped to the ground unharmed. More than 30 people died.

WHAT iT FEELS LiKE...

... TO BE BURiED iN AN AVALANCHE

Lester Morlang, 49, contractor

We were at 12,700ft, putting a snowshed over a goldmine in the La Plato Mountains in Colorado. It was about four o'clock. My colleague Jack was handing me some 12ft planks. There was no warning: it was instant. All of a sudden I was curled up in a ball doing somersaults. Then it was over and I was buried. They figured out later I was buried under 50 feet of snow. It was totally dark. My mouth was packed with snow. The pressure was enormous; it was hard to breathe. I didn't know which direction was up. I thought, 'Oh my God, am I going to die like this?' And then I thought, 'Maybe I'm already dead.'

Luckily I had my hands over my face. I cleared the snow out of my mouth with my fingers. And then I was screaming for Jack. You get into something like this and you absolutely lose it. It was absolute panic. I was screaming, I was bawling, I was out of my mind. The tears and snot and stuff were flowing. And then I noticed it: all the tears were kind of running crossways across my face. I realised I was lying kind of upside down and backwards. That was a real moment of truth. Now I had a mission. I had to get out.

I moved my hands around, compacting the snow, giving myself a little more room. Then I got my upper body loose, and I started digging. I made a little game of it. I'd count to four, and then I'd reach up and grab a handful of snow. I'd pull it past my face, past my chest, down to my knees. And then with my knees I would kind of push it down to my feet and stomp it down. I dug like that for 22 hours, and then I broke through. I pushed my hand out and saw the first little bit of light, and I was jubilant. I screamed and hollered and thanked the Lord. It was another 14 hours before the rescuers found me. The whole experience has made me a better person. Trivial things don't bother me any more. I can smash my finger or something, and sometimes I'll just giggle thinking how great it is to smash my finger. I guess I see a few things now that a regular person doesn't.

...TO BE BITTEN BY A SHARK

Rodney Orr, 63, electrician

I was on my paddleboard in the Pacific near Santa Rosa, California. I was getting ready to dive off the side and go spearfishing when the lights went out. I heard this loud noise like a garage door slamming, and it was completely dark. Then all of a sudden I could see these big white things out of my left eye. At first I thought it was broken Fibreglass. I thought maybe a boat had run over me and stuffed by head through my board. But as soon as I touched the white things, I realised that they were teeth. A shark had a hold of my head.

I was at a right angle to its mouth, hanging out the side. The front teeth were buried in my cheekbone and my nose. It was quick and sharp. The teeth were like razors. When he clamped on to me, it was a God-awful crunch. I heard the crunching and the teeth plough through the bone, but it didn't hurt. Something in the brain clicks so you don't feel it till later. He didn't take me down – he took me out of the water. When I saw the water, it was like three feet below, but I could see we were moving fast. I reached up to the shark and it was flat, like the side of a Buick, and it had a kind of sandpapery feel. And then I just started pounding on it. I went beserk. I shredded my gloves on his teeth. I was just striking at him blind. I don't know if that's what made him let go of me. If he had finished the bite, I would have had no brain.

When the thing let go, it went underneath me. It was a great white; wider than my shoulders. It had a hold of me for eight to 12 seconds. We probably travelled about 60 to 70 feet. I swam back to my board, blood pouring out of my nose, out of my face. I couldn't feel anything from the top of my head to my bum on the right side. I had a two-inch hole in the back of my neck. I was choking and spitting out all this blood that was running down the back of my throat. And I said, 'I gotta get to shore. Now.'

From *What It Feels Like*, edited by A.J. Jacobs

They took me in a helicopter to Santa Rosa hospital. I had 35 or 40 stitches in the front and 25 or 30 in the back. They had no mirrors at the hospital. The only glimpse I caught was a reflection in the helicopter window. I looked like hamburger. Now, I've got one bad scar near the corner of my eye and my nose; but hell, they've faded and fit with the wrinkles.

TEXT H

Shark Practice

A sudden spate of attacks by sharks has struck terror into Florida's tourists this summer. Except, that is, among the thrill-seeking few who have been actively initiating close encounters with the creatures – and, allegedly, encouraging the attacks by doing so. The result? A ferocious row, and a hair-raising investigative assignment for **David Usborne ...**

As Jeff Torode manoeuvred his scuba-diving boat out from its dock one recent afternoon, he did the equivalent of those last-minute destination checks that you sometimes get on aeroplanes. 'We are on a shark dive today. Everyone does know that, right? Anyone who needs to go back, say so now!' You would think that every last one of would have screamed to be let off. But no, we nodded at him and smiled.

So there we were, 38 apparently sane souls heading out to the open ocean off the coast of Florida in search of the one species of fish normal people would very much like never to see, unless in an aquarium. There were some serious diving folk fiddling ceaselessly with the tubes and valves on their oxygen bottles, and then there were mums and dads and kids. There was Martin, 40, for example, a teacher from Ramsgate, Kent, and an experienced diver. He had left his wife back at the hotel, 'checking my life insurance policy'. But there was also Jacob, from Fort Myers, who was 12.

Jacob, it turned out, had done this before and knew the drill. Once tied to our buoy half a mile from the shore at Pompano Beach, just north of Fort Lauderdale, we would all plop in the water and head to the sea-bed 15ft. below. Jeff, the skipper and part-owner of the South Florida Diving Headquarters, the scuba diving

outfit running the trip, would get everyone sitting in a semicircle to wait for Scot. Those not certified – me and one other guy – would stay on the surface with snorkel gear. Scot Dickerson was the shark-feeder, who would make sure we got what we had come for – a close encounter with a shark. 'I was scared at first. But once you get down there, it's awesome,' Jacob said, trying to reassure me.

It was kind of the kid, but it didn't work. There are lots of ways to explore the frontiers of your fear, and, frankly, I am not fond of any of them. I remained especially baffled, however, by the appeal of shark-feeding, which has become one of the fastest-growing attractions here in South Florida and in the nearby Bahamas. Just recently, it has also turned into one of the most controversial tourist activities. Florida has seen a spate of highly-publicised shark attacks recently, and some people are beginning to see a connection between the attacks and the suddenly popular shark-feeding safaris like the one I was taking.

However, details of the debate, which has prompted some state politicians to try to ban shark-feeding altogether, were not uppermost in my mind as I got into the water. 'Jeff, got the morphine on board?' one of the more macho divers piped up, attempting morbid humour. Moments later, as I bobbed around and fretted about my mask fogging up, Jeff appeared alongside me with interesting news. 'Look, there's one down there already,' he said breezily. And with that he vanished beneath the waves. There it was. The fearful outline of its fins and snout were unmistakable. Silently cruising right underneath me was a grown nurse shark that was perhaps eight feet long. I reacted in several ways. I started to giggle and to breathe very fast. I was also overcome with a desperate need to pee in the water, but wondered if I should. The merest whiff of urine, it occurred to me, might send the sharks into a feeding frenzy. Above all, I started to wonder what I would have done, had I been alone with that fish. The answer was

obvious: I would have thrashed about madly, screamed my lungs out and had a heart attack.

Nurse sharks are docile and rarely bother humans. Indeed, most species of shark will leave us alone, unless we somehow antagonise or threaten them. 'Humans are not on their menu,' was how Torode put it. The Great Whites are the obvious exception. But right at that moment, none of that soothing science mattered to me. Nor was I impressed with the statistic that says you are more likely to be struck by lightning than eaten by a shark. My mind was filling with images from *Jaws*, the 1975 horror epic by Steven Spielberg, with its awful, two-note score – 'Ta-duh, tah-duh' – and the slogan 'Don't go in the water'. I was in the water already and there was a shark right underneath me. No wonder I was giggling.

But then, instead of sheer panic, curiosity took hold of me. I forced my breathing to slow down and turned my gaze below to watch Scot drawing five sharks into the semicircle of divers. They came to him, obviously, because of the food of bloody morsels of fish called chum, packed into a short PVC tube that he held in his right hand. For 30 minutes he strung the sharks along, allowing them only occasional slurps at the pipe. (Nurse sharks have blunt teeth and suck the flesh from their victims – another Torode titbit that I had not found entirely reassuring.) We had been instructed to avoid touching the sharks but, of course, nearly everyone succumbed to the temptation to reach out and discover what a shark feels like.

Up on the surface, looking down, we snorkellers remained mere spectators. Shortly before finishing, however, Scot remembered us and brought the tube of chum – and the sharks – up towards us. I dived down to meet them. And suddenly, there I was, face to face with the largest of the sharks. Its eyes and mine seem to lock for a second and, had I wanted to, I, too, could have touched it. But suddenly I choked on a surge of adrenalin and rushed to the surface, lungs bursting …

From the *Independent*, 1 September 2001, by David Usborne

In thirty-five feet of water, the great fish swam slowly, its tail waving just enough to maintain motion. It saw nothing, for the water was murky with motes of vegetation. The fish had been moving parallel to the shoreline. Now it turned, banking slightly, and followed the bottom gradually upward. The fish perceived more light in the water, but still it saw nothing.

The boy was resting, his arms dangling down, his feet and ankles dipping in and out of the water with each small swell. His head was turned towards shore, and he noticed that he had been carried out beyond what his mother would consider safe. He could see her lying on her towel, and the man and child playing in the wavewash. He was not afraid, for the water was calm and he wasn't really very far from shore – only forty yards or so. But he wanted to get closer; otherwise his mother might sit up, spy him, and order him out of the water. He eased himself back a little bit so he could use his feet to help propel himself. He began to kick and paddle towards shore. His arms displaced water almost silently, but his kicking feet made erratic splashes and left swirls of bubbles in his wake.

The fish did not hear the sound, but rather registered the sharp and jerky impulses emitted by the kicks. They were signals, faint but true, and the fish locked on them, homing. It rose, slowly at first, then gaining speed as the signals grew stronger.

The boy stopped for a moment to rest. The signals ceased. The fish slowed, turning its head from side to side, trying to recover them. The boy lay perfectly still, and the fish passed beneath him, skimming the sandy bottom. Again it turned.

The boy resumed paddling. He kicked only every third or fourth stroke; kicking was more exertion than steady paddling. But the occasional kicks sent new signals to the fish. This time it needed to lock on them only an instant, for it was almost directly below the boy.

The fish rose. Nearly vertical, it now saw the commotion on the surface. There was no conviction that what thrashed above was food, but food was not a concept of significance. The fish was impelled to attack: if what it swallowed was digestible, that was food; if not, it would later be regurgitated. The mouth opened, and with a final sweep of the sickle tail the fish struck.

The boy's last – only – thought was that he had been punched in the stomach. The breath was driven from him in a sudden rush. He had no time to cry out, nor, had he had the time, would he have known what to cry, for he could not see the fish. The fish's head drove the raft out of the water. The jaws smashed together, engulfing head, arms, shoulders, trunk, pelvis and most of the raft. Nearly half the fish had come clear of the water, and it slid forward and down in a belly-flopping motion, grinding the mass of flesh and bone and rubber. The boy's legs were severed at the hip, and they sank, spinning slowly to the bottom.

From Jaws *by Peter Benchley*

1 Look back at the extracts in Text G.
   a) Which account do you find most powerful?
   b) Explain how the writer of your chosen account draws the reader in (think about the narrative voice, the vocabulary, the description of events and emotions).

2 Think back to your own worst ever experience – it might be a car crash, getting lost from a parent, being stuck in a cupboard. Imagine a TV show called 'Personal Horror', based on A.J. Jacobs's book. In small groups, enact an interview on the show about someone's worst experience. One person should take on the role of the host, another the interviewee, and the rest the audience.

Host:
   ✦ Plan your questions, but be flexible enough to respond sensitively to what your guest says.
   ✦ Try to discover not only what happened, but also what it felt like.
   ✦ Write down some prompts if you need to (e.g. five questions), but try to use these as little as possible. Instead, make eye-contact with your guest, talk to her or him informally, taking real interest in the tale she/he tells.

Guest:
   ✦ Think about your story but listen to the questions asked by the host. Answer the questions with as much detail as possible.
   ✦ Use language to convey the feelings you experienced at the time of your nightmare event.

Audience:
   ✦ Watch the way the host and guest interact.
   ✦ Listen to the quality of the host's questions: are they open-ended and designed to encourage the guest to talk? Does the host actively listen to the guest's responses and respond appropriately?
   ✦ How could the host and guest improve their use of language?

3 Text H contains personal and factual information. Copy and complete the grid below, filling in what you learn about the writer and about sharks.

Writer	Sharks

54

4 Text H gives a detailed account of the writer's personal experience. Think about how it might be different if it were the opening of a novel. Write the first couple of paragraphs of a fictional version of the text.

5 Look more closely at Text I.
  a) Why do you think the writer refers to the shark as 'the fish'?
  b) Why does he call the victim 'the boy' rather than give him a name?
  c) How does the writer use paragraphing to build suspense?
  d) Look at the language of paragraph 5. Which of these words best describes it: detached, scientific, emotive, technical, detailed? Be prepared to justify your response.

6 Plot the levels of tension in the text on a graph, paragraph by paragraph. It should clearly show which paragraph has the highest level of tension and which has the lowest. Compare your graph with a friend's.

High

Medium

Low

Level of tension

Paragraph   1   2   3   4   5   6

7 Discuss and compare your responses to Texts G, H and I. Which text did you find:
  a) most interesting?
  b) least interesting?
  c) most informative?
  d) least informative?

Be ready to justify your response with reference to the relevant text.

EXTREME NATURE

Sometimes we view nature as gentle, charming and attractive – think of rolling landscapes and Disney images of puppies and kittens. Nature can also be raw, powerful and unforgiving – think of hurricanes, storms and food chains.

 The poet Ted Hughes is well known for his celebration of the merciless power of nature. Compare his poem (Text J) describing a walk through a field of sheep with a much earlier poem by William Blake (Text K).

 Before you read, discuss with a partner:
+ If you were asked to write a poem about sheep or lambs, what kind of poem would you expect to write?
+ What kind of images might you expect to include?

Ravens
by Ted Hughes

As we came through the gate to look at the few new lambs
On the skyline of lawn smoothness,
A raven bundled itself into air from midfield
And slid away under hard glistenings, low and guilty.
Sheep nibbling, kneeling to nibble the reluctant nibbled grass.   5
Sheep staring, their jaws pausing to think, then chewing again,
Then pausing. Over there a new lamb
Just getting up, bumping its mother's nose
As she nibbles the sugar coating off it
While the tattered banners of her triumph swing and drip from her rear-end.   10
She sneezes and a glim of water flashes from her rear-end.
She sneezes again and again, till she's emptied.
She carries on investigating her new present and seeing how it works.
Over here is something else. But you are still interested
In that new one, and its new spark of voice,   15
And its tininess.
Now over here, where the raven was,
Is what interests you next. Born dead,
Twisted like a scarf, a lamb of an hour or two,
Its insides, the various jellies and crimsons and transparencies   20
And threads and tissues pulled out
In straight lines, like tent ropes
From its upward belly opened like a lamb-wool slipper,
The fine anatomy of silvery ribs on display and the cavity,
The head also emptied through the eye-sockets,   25
The woolly limbs swathed in birth-yolk and impossible

To tell now which in all this field of quietly nibbling sheep
Was its mother. I explain
That it died being born. We should have been here, to help it.
So it died being born. 'And did it cry?' you cry.   30
I pick up the dangling greasy weight by the hooves soft as dogs' pads
That had trodden only womb-water
And its raven-drawn strings dangle and trail,
Its loose head joggles, and 'Did it cry?' you cry again.
Its two-fingered feet splay in their skin between the pressures   35
Of my fingers and thumb. And there is another,
Just born, all black, splaying its tripod, inching its new points
Towards its mother, and testing the note
It finds in its mouth. But you have eyes now
Only for the tattered bundle of throwaway lamb.   40
'Did it cry?' you keep asking, in a three-year-old field-wide
Piercing persistence. 'Oh yes' I say 'it cried'.

Though this one was lucky insofar
As it made the attempt into a warm wind
And its first day of death was blue and warm   45
The magpies gone quiet with domestic happiness
And skylarks not worrying about anything
And the blackthorn budding confidently
And the skyline of hills, after millions of hard years,
Sitting soft.

TEXT K

The Lamb
by William Blake

Little Lamb, who made thee?
　Does thou know who made thee,
Gave thee life and bid thee feed
By the stream and o'er the mead;
Gave thee clothing of delight,
Softest clothing woolly bright;
Gave thee such a tender voice,
Making all the vales rejoice?
　Little Lamb who made thee?
　Does thou know who made thee?

Little Lamb I'll tell thee,
　Little Lamb I'll tell thee:
He is called by thy name,
For he calls himself a lamb.
He is meek and he is mild;
He became a little child.
I a child and thou a lamb,
We are callèd by his name.
　Little Lamb God bless thee.
　Little Lamb God bless thee.

ACTIVITIES

1 Think carefully about how the lambs are presented in the poems.

   a) Draw two pictures: one to represent each poem.

   b) Discuss the images, explaining how they relate to the poems.

2 First look back at Text K.

   a) Which ideas and images are the sort you would expect in a poem about a lamb?

   b) Do any of its images surprise you?

3 Text J contains some surprising words and images. Look at the list below. Choose five of them and comment on the image they create in your mind and why the writer might have chosen them.

Line	Word or image	Comment
3	A raven bundled itself into air	
5	Sheep nibbling … nibble	
9	She nibbles the sugar coating off it	
10	The tattered banners of her triumph swing and drip from her rear-end	
20	Its insides, the various jellies and crimsons and transparencies	
21/22	And threads and tissues pulled out in straight lines, like tent ropes	
26	The woolly limbs swathed in birth-yolk	
37	Splaying its tripod	

4 'Ravens' is a poem in two sections: first the narrative about walking through the fields and seeing the lambs; secondly the final eight lines in which the writer says that the dead lamb was 'lucky'. Try to explain his argument.

UNIT CHALLENGES

1. Impersonal writing

Write a commentary on Ted Hughes' poem 'Ravens'. Guide a reader through it, commenting on:

a) what happens (the content)

b) how the poem is written (the style).

✦ An impersonal style uses the third person, not the first-person pronouns 'I' and 'me'. However, you can use a personal style for the last paragraph of your commentary in which you say what you like or dislike about the poem.

✦ Use short quotations.

✦ Use a variety of sentences – complex and simple – to give variety to your work.

✦ Use colons to introduce quotations and examples. For example: 'The early part of the poem immediately creates a feeling of menace: a raven looks "guilty".'

✦ Use semi-colons to separate different but related clauses in a sentence. For example: 'the poem celebrates new life; it also shows us that death is just as natural.'

✦ Check that your handwriting is neat and legible. If the reader has to struggle to read it, the impact of the content is lost!

2. Personal writing

In his book, *What It Feels Like…*, A.J. Jacobs uses accounts of various unpleasant experiences by different people. Think back to one of the worst moments in your life. It could be:

✦ an accident
✦ getting into trouble
✦ making a terrible mistake
✦ getting lost
✦ hearing some bad news.

Write a personal account of this bad experience, describing what happened, how you felt, and why you think the incident had such an effect.

Make your description come to life with:

✦ vivid vocabulary which excites various senses (e.g. sight, sound and smell)
✦ active verbs (instead of 'it was raining' say 'the rain hammered onto the earth')
✦ a range of sentence types.

Punctuation:

✦ Use colons to build your reader's expectations. For example, 'I felt at that point that things couldn't get any worse: they did.'

✦ Use semi-colons to separate different but related clauses in a sentence. For example, 'The sun was beating down; the birds were singing; the day should have been perfect.'

3. Horror story

Jaws is one of the most famous novels about humans clashing with nature. It was part of a trend of movies that examined what happened when nature seemed to turn against humans (others were *Earthquake*, *Killer Bees*, *Piranha*).

Think of your own tale of a natural horror (e.g. an unstoppable swarm of ants, an invasion of rats, a sea filled with jellyfish).

Write the opening sequence of a novel about your chosen horror. It should hint about what might happen, but not reveal the true scale and terror of it. Remember that you need to:
✦ grab the reader's attention
✦ convey a sense of danger
✦ build up some tension and suspense.

ASSESS YOUR LEARNING

● Adapt your talk to different contexts with increasing confidence
● Take an active part in discussion, showing understanding of ideas and sensitivity

Review how your spoken language is developing.
a) Think about the feedback you had from the audience of the interview (on page 54).
b) Draw up a grid listing your strengths and weaknesses in spoken English. Consider how well you are improving in the following areas:
    ✦ listening
    ✦ speaking clearly, fluently, sufficiently loud
    ✦ matching your language to the audience and topic
    ✦ encouraging others.

● Identify different layers of meaning and comment on their significance and effect
● Summarize a range of information from different sources

You have read a number of complex texts in this unit.
a) Give yourself a * to ***** rating for how well you have:
    ✦ been able to find key ideas in texts

✦ read texts to identify specific points
✦ compared the different features of texts
✦ quoted important parts of a text's language
✦ commented on the writer's use of language.

b) Which skill(s) do you need to practise more?

c) What kind of activity might help you to develop your reading?

● Adapt your style and register to different forms, including an impersonal style

● Write in a neat, legible form

● Use a range of punctuation to clarify meaning

a) What do you think are the three most important ingredients in an impersonal style of writing?

b) Look back at your commentary on the 'Ravens' poem. Is it clear and legible? Give it to a partner and ask her or him how easy or difficult it is to read.

c) Write a quick description for each of these punctuation marks showing that you understand what its key function is:

Full stop (.)
Comma (,)
Colon (:)
Semi-colon (;)

FINISHING LINE

Imagine that you work for a travel company that markets the 'ultimate extreme experiences'. So far you have come up with:

✦ scuba-diving in a cage in the Caribbean – in shark-infested water
✦ a giant game of hide-and-seek in the labyrinths on Crete
✦ parachuting into an unknown location (e.g. desert) which you have to find your way out of (satellite tracking system provided)

Think of another couple of ideas. Decide which might be possible, and which are simply too foolhardy. Then brainstorm a slogan that might be used in marketing one of the ideas.

Identity crisis

Learning objectives

By the end of this unit you should be able to:

- Adapt your talk to different contexts with increasing confidence
- Engage your listener with a variety of expressions and vocabulary
- Use standard English with fluency

- Identify different layers of meaning and comment on their significance and effect
- Give a personal and critical response to thematic, structural and linguistic features in literature

- Write confidently showing appropriate choices of style in a range of forms
- Develop characters and settings in narrative writing

INTRODUCTION

This unit is about who we are and who we would like to be. It includes magazine articles about being famous, and an advice text on how to get on TV. The final extract is a short story about a girl's desperate attempt to break out of the identity she has been given.

WARM-UP

1   In medieval times, it was widely believed that four body fluids controlled your temperament and personality. These were known as the four humours:

- blood (Latin word *sanguinis*, meaning bloody)
- phlegm (Greek word meaning 'to burn')
- choler (Greek word meaning bile – the substance in the pit of your stomach)
- melancholy (Greek *melas*, meaning black and *chole*, meaning bile).

Using the chart opposite, look at what the humours are supposed to say about our personalities and what is associated with each humour. With a partner, decide which personality description fits you best.

Sanguine	Phlegmatic	Choleric	Melancholic
Affable, brave, good-humoured, not easily offended, open-minded	Slow moving, timid, mild, not easily angered	Passionate, shows emotions, quick to anger, strong, reckless, a leader	Quick-witted, calculating, brooding, holds grudges, determined, moody
Warm and moist	Cold and moist	Hot and dry	Cold and dry
Adolescence	Senility/childhood	Adulthood	Old age
South	East	West	North
Air	Water	Fire	Earth
Spring	Winter	Summer	Autumn
Jupiter	Moon	Mars	Saturn
Gemini, Libra, Aquarius	Taurus, Virgo, Capricorn	Aries, Leo, Sagittarius	Cancer, Scorpio, Pisces

2 Some people take their star sign or horoscope very seriously, believing that it helps to explain their personality. Look at these two views and discuss your own perspective.

View 1:

We know that the moon has a powerful effect on the weather, the tides, the cycles of our bodies. Why shouldn't other planets have similar effects? Since we are more than 85% water, no wonder the planets influence us so much.

View 2:

It's nonsense to suggest that you can divide everyone in the human race into 12 categories and assume they will have similar personalities and fortune. Only a fool would bother to read such nonsense.

3   Read the five sound bites below. They include lyrics and quotations.

Fame!
I'm gonna live forever.
I'm gonna learn how to fly,
High!
I feel it coming together,
People will see me and cry
Fame!
I'm going to make it to heaven,
Light up the sky like a flame,
Fame!
I'm gonna live forever,
Baby remember my name,
Remember, Remember, Remember,
Remember, Remember, Remember.

Lyrics by Michael Gore and Dean Pitchford,
from the film *Fame*

II

He who pursues fame at the risk of losing his self is not a scholar.

Chuang-tzu (369 to 286 BC)

Fame lost its appeal for me when I went into a public restroom and an autograph seeker handed me a pen and paper under the stall door.

Marlo Thomas

Without relationships, no matter how much wealth, fame, power, prestige and seeming success by the standards and opinions of the world one has, happiness will constantly elude one.

Sidney Madwed

V

What is fame? The advantage of being known by people of whom you yourself know nothing, and for whom you care as little.

Stanislaus

a) How do the lyrics of the song (sound bite I) suggest the desperation to be famous?
b) Why do you think that so many people want to be famous nowadays?
c) What is your own attitude to fame?
d) Which quotation do you like the most and why?
e) Do you think the media has made fame too easy? Can you be famous without any talent whatsoever?

FAME

The following three texts are about different aspects of fame: Text A gives advice on how to become a TV presenter; Text B is a newspaper article about the price of fame; Text C looks at how famous people behave. Read the texts, thinking about the advantages and disadvantages of fame.

The Break into TV

How do you get into presentation work on television? Gatecrash the right parties? Bribe producers? Sell your soul?

The first thing to remember is that a TV station is not a forbidden planet and you don't need written permission just to walk into reception. Forget any glamorous image and imagine it to be what it is … a place of work. If you can do a job that needs to be done, they'll pay you for it; it's as simple as that. The hardest thing is to get your first break, which you'll achieve through a knowledge of the jobs around, through the effective communication of your talent to the right people, and through persistence, ingenuity, and a bit of luck.

Presenters' jobs are advertised rarely, and then often only as a sop to management to prove there's nobody better than the producer's original choice. Sometimes a TV station has a stable of presenters who are assigned jobs in the news and various regional shows by a head of department. If this is the case, you will have to discover, through your dealings, who actually hires and fires talent. Producers may have their hands tied here when it comes to choosing presenters.

If the programme makers have free rein, it's open season, so go for it. Find out their names, and suggest new features. Don't criticise their existing presenters, but mention how your unique style could add an extra dimension to the show. Badger, but don't pester. Explain your ideas, but don't ramble. The average producer is a tormented individual who has to juggle many balls in the air. Your letters will go straight in the bin unless you can show you've got something to offer.

When there's news in the air that a programme is looking for presenters, the producer is suddenly snowed under with tapes and CVs, usually from faceless agents. That's why your taking a personal, individual approach is much more likely to bear fruit than your staying at home and hoping an agent will do all the work for you. In any case, agents will only

65

take you on if you've a decent track record behind you, or if you can prove you really are very special.

There is no magic formula that will help you achieve your first break in TV. There are as many different experiences as there are presenters, but in every case it all boils down to having talent, ability and that vital, elusive factor: luck.

Annie McKie is a co-presenter of the BBC TV regional news programme from Bristol, *News West*. Her break came from a case of mistaken identity. 'I always wanted to be a performer. After graduating from drama school in London, life on stage as an actress was very exciting but also very uncertain.' Annie put herself on the market as a corporate video presenter using her real name, Annie Rice. 'One of the clients booked me thinking I was *Anneka* Rice – and on the day wondered where the long blonde hair and jumpsuit was! In the end I presented the video to everyone's satisfaction and was given more and more work.'

Annie used extracts of her corporate video work to compile a show-tape which eventually led to work as a newsreader and presenter for BBC TV's regional programmes for the West Country. She also hosts radio programmes for the BBC and this is where she feels potential TV presenters can most effectively learn their basic skills. 'My advice to newcomers is to get any job in radio, do it very, very well – never complain – come up with ideas of your own and somehow make yourself indispensable. You have got to offer more than you're asked to do. Radio teaches you about getting the voice right, timing, editing and editorial skills which of course all apply in television work too. Above all, never be complacent – you've got to stay one step ahead of everyone else. Keep you eyes and ears open so you will be in the best possible position to take advantage of any opportunities which come your way.'

At twenty-six, Toby Anstis is well established at BBC TV as one of the main faces of children's programming. 'I knew I wanted to go into television when I was at school but I came up against a barrage of negativity. I started doing hospital radio when I was fourteen and got the bug – for me, presenting is all about sharing ideas and things that interest you with other people. I did a degree in Marketing and Psychology and started working in a marketing job in London during the week while doing some presenting on a local cable radio network at the weekends.

'My big break came when I put a show reel together while working at the cable station and sent it to the BBC. They said they would see me so I went in and within two hours they had offered me a six-month contract.'

From *Making it as a Radio or TV Presenter* by Peter Baker

TEXT **B**

Anyone can be famous – but the price is high
by Sarfraz Manzoor

1 'You got big dreams? You want fame? Well, fame costs, and right here is where you start paying.' Back in the 80s, it was with those stirring words that the American television series *Fame* would begin each week. For those who do not remember it, or have successfully expunged it from their memories, the series was based around the lives and ambitions of the students of the New York City High School for the Performing Arts. The young dancers, singers and actors were taught that the price of fame was paid in sweat. Hard work was the way to earn fame, that was how you got them to remember your name; sweat and elaborate song-and-dance numbers on the streets of New York City.

2 Earning fame? Doesn't that just sound so last century? We might have always wanted to be famous, rich and beautiful but until recently it was only the province of those blessed with the right talent, genes or connections. Today, fame, fortune and beauty (albeit of the fake plastic variety) can be achieved with far greater speed and ease: by simply appearing on a reality television series. The huge number of such programmes means the currency of celebrity has become cheaper, yet the price of fame has, perversely, increased. Twenty years on from *Fame*, aspiring celebrities need to be prepared to pay their dues not in sweat but in the pain of cosmetic surgery and shamelessness.

3 That is a lesson the contestants of the latest series of *Big Brother*, which returns next week, will learn the hard way. Those who apply to go on such shows want to become famous, and they are prepared to pay the price of sacrificing their privacy and dignity.

4 The new series of the grandaddy of reality television shows starts on the same evening as the final episode of *Friends* (which stars former New York City High School for the Performing Arts student, Jennifer Aniston), and Channel 4 claims that this is the year that Big Brother gets 'evil'. Given the context, 'evil' presumably does not mean that the housemates will be required to ritually sacrifice the chickens; instead we can expect the contestants to be given tasks and challenges that are likely to cause tensions and conflicts. This year's darker *Big Brother* is the television bosses' response to the studied benignity of last year's housemates. They thought that by being inoffensive, and refusing to offer the controversy and drama expected of them they could beat the system – i.e. gain fame while retaining their dignity. But the viewers and the press want blood not banality. As their subsequent non-careers have demonstrated, in the end the House always wins.

5 One person who knows all about shamelessness is Jordan. 'Her desire to be famous was not as easy a path to take as one might imagine. It involved great strength of mind to overcome the challenges she faced in her early life, and get rid of the self-doubt you could forgive her for suffering.' These are the words of one reviewer on Amazon talking about the pneumatic sex icon's autobiography, *Being Jordan*. Its extraordinary success … has even led to the startling claim that Jordan is a good role model for young women.

6 But before she was Jordan she was Katie Price, and cosmetic surgery was the price to be paid for turning Katie into Jordan. With Jordan as a poster girl for the wonders of how surgery can transform one's fortunes, it isn't surprising others want to follow her. Why bother with singing lessons or writing courses when a succession of cosmetic surgical procedures can deliver the same rewards?

7 That, I think, is why contestants willingly appear on shows such as *Extreme Makeover* and MTV's *I Want a Famous Face*: they believe that with some drastic plastic surgery, they too can have the lifestyle that might otherwise involve a lot of hard work …

8 What I find most fascinating about the rise of this form of programming is what it tells us about the changing role of television in people's lives. Once it was merely the box in the corner of the living room that sought to educate, inform and entertain. That is not enough now. Today's programme makers want shows that make an impact, that inspire change – be it by renovating old buildings, improving the diets of schoolchildren or creating pop idols. Television has evolved from being merely a window on to the world, into something that seeks to enable change.

9 That desire can partly be explained in strategic terms; in a more fragmented and promiscuous viewing environment, programme makers need to find more effective ways to reach audiences, and making things bigger and more ambitious is one way of doing that. But there is, I think, another reason. According to a new series – *The Rise of the Celebrity Class*, which begins on Saturday on BBC2 – celebrities represent a modern version of the aristocracy. If that is true, and it seems at least plausible, then it is television that is the kingmaker; the programme makers recognizing and enjoying their power to create celebrities.

10 It was Jordan's appearance on *I'm a Celebrity – Get Me Out of Here!* that helped soften her public image, and I can't help thinking there must have been an element of sadistic glee when the programme makers realized they could persuade Jordan to eat worms on national television. They will be emitting similar misanthropic chuckles, no doubt, when the new *Big Brother* contestants are allowed to humiliate themselves on live television – on the off-chance that, once the series is over, they might secure an appearance on *Win, Lose or Draw*.

11 Programmes such as *Big Brother* are like a dirty dance conducted in public between those who want fame and those who can bestow it – but it is danced to television's theme tune. Perhaps it is true that 20 years ago fame could be earned with hard work and sweat, but today, while the opportunities for fame are greater, the deal that television strikes is a far tougher one. As they prepare themselves for their first brush with fame and notoriety, the contestants of *Big Brother* would do well to remember that fame still costs, and the instant the camera light turns red is the moment you start paying.

From the *Guardian*, 19 May 2004

TEXT C

Ways to be a travel diva

Grand pianos, personal gyms, ceiling mirrors and island bookings. Celebrity travel has no limits to the 'Me, me, me' demands, says *Rupert Mellor*.

Celebrities. They're just like you and me, you know. They eat, sleep, use the bathroom facilities, and when they get time off, just like us they like a bit of peace and quiet.

'What the really famous prize is total privacy,' says hotel guru Nigel Massey. 'The Julia Robertses, the Bruce Willises, the Richard Geres – they spend their money getting away. George Clooney has a stock answer if he's recognised – 'No, I'm not him, but a lot of people say that.' All you read about J-Lo demanding the air around her be scented with gardenia, is all massively exaggerated, or made up by stars' publicists for the sake of newspaper space.'

Yeah, yeah, yeah … But hoteliers, travel agents, pet pamperers and others on the 'divas' demands' frontline have other stories to tell.

1) Travel with entourage, pointless staff and excess(ive) baggage
To celebrate his 33rd birthday in November 2002, P Diddy, the artist formerly known as Puff Daddy, flew 300 close pals, including Naomi Campbell, Gerard Depardieu and Ivana Trump, on chartered jets from New York and Paris to Marrakesh for five days of unbridled ostentation. The tab? $1 million, including the brolly-wallah paid to shade the king of bling.

While Whitney Houston employs an assistant to walk into hotel rooms ahead of her to check the temperature, and to test her bathwater with a thermometer, our own Queen is trying to pare down her image as a big spender. But behind the scenes lie some definite diva complexes. The Queen once arrived at the Sheraton hotel in Durban with one meagre piece of baggage, but two tons of luggage arrived later, and staff had already been given a six-page document, detailing everything from the right type of notepaper for her desk to how her bed should be made – sheets and blankets, not duvets, turned down exactly nine inches below the eiderdown. Mauve blooms and carnations were royally banished from bouquets; TVs in the bedroom, bloody meat and spicy food were all ruled out, and she would only drink Malvern mineral water – her own supply.

2) Never be satisfied with your suite
For Sylvester Stallone, the travel essential was an extra room – when he, his family and nanny checked in to the Fairmont Chateau, the most prestigious hotel in Whistler, Canada, he gave instructions to clear it to make way for a private gym. What baffled hotel staff was the amount of time the *Rocky* star spent 'posing in the hotel's health club', when he had all the equipment in his suite …

The need to stay camera-friendly prompts plenty a personal spec. Staff at London's Carlton Tower on Sloane Street report a very famous guest who had his room converted into a gym so he could pump iron unobserved. Whether it was the same guest who asked for a mirror on the ceiling above his bed, they are too discreet to reveal.

However the mirror man also sent ahead framed pictures of himself to be hung on the walls of his room, and asked for the initials of his lady friend to be embroidered onto the bathrobes. By the time he arrived, the hotel had prepared three pairs of bathrobes, each with a different set of initials, as he had changed his mind three times about who to bring.

'Cher had a particular request when she stayed with us,' says Ondrej Stefek, communications manager at Prague's 1930s gem, the Radisson SAS Alcron Hotel. 'She likes to play the piano, and asked if we could move a concert grand into the Presidential Apartment, her suite, on the seventh floor. One lorry delivery, a crane hoist and a hasty retune later, the veteran diva was all set. 'It was no trouble at all,' breezes Stefek. 'We were very happy to help,' although he'll admit that Cher was more demanding than his other music megastar guest at the time, 'simply because Marilyn Manson could not have been quieter. He was a very nice man.'...

3) Designer downshift

Harrison Ford may have made headlines recently, photographed with girlfriend Calista Flockhart steering a narrowboat on our very own Oswestry canal. But back in the superstar's spiritual home, the US – where fear of terrorism has seen a surge of domestic holidaying – a new, parallel leisure trend is emerging. Four hours' drive north of Manhattan, the mountain and lake-strewn Adirondacks are quietly replacing the Hamptons as the celebrities' East Coast idyll, where the super-rich can get back to the unfeasibly expensive land.

Ford has a place here near West Port, while Sigourney Weaver's discreet Long Lake weekend home is close at hand. But even the arrival by private jet of Britney Spears and Justin Timberlake three years ago to celebrate her 20th birthday barely dented the getting-away-from-it-all calm.

It's a direction mirrored in the rolling hills of Litchfield County, Connecticut. Sometimes nicknamed Beverley Hills East, the area is becoming characterised by the A-list farmers – Ralph Lauren, Mia Farrow, Dustin Hoffman, Kevin Bacon – whose only demand is to holiday like simple folk, in their multi-million dollar homes. Never mind that locals smirk and call them, behind their backs, the mink and manure set.

1 Many people are attracted to the idea of being famous. Texts A to C show different views of fame. With a partner, draw up a list of the advantages and disadvantages of fame, supporting each point with a quotation from one of the texts.

2 Look closely at Text A and the way it is structured. Design a graph (either as a bar chart or pie chart) which shows what proportions you think are:
   + advice (e.g. what you should do to get noticed)
   + description (e.g. what producers do)
   + examples (e.g. people who are now working in television)

3 Which parts of Text A did you find:
   a) helpful
   b) interesting
   c) obvious?

4 Now look at the way Text A is written.

   a) Why do you think the byline starts with questions rather than statements?

   b) Look at paragraph 3. Many of the writer's sentences are commands rather than statements or questions. Choose four examples and explain why you think the writer chose to write in this style.

5 Text B is an opinion piece written in 11 paragraphs. Explore the way the writer constructs his argument and the tone he adopts, using this grid:

Paragraph	Main point	Tone (funny, sarcastic, rude)
1		
2		
3		
4		
5		
6		
7		
8		
9		
10		
11		

6 Discuss which of the statements a to e below you agree with about Text B. For each statement decide whether you:

   ✦ completely agree (CA)

   ✦ mostly agree (MA)

   ✦ mostly disagree (MD)

   ✦ completely disagree (CD)

   ✦ not sure (NS).

   a) The writer's tone is sometimes too sarcastic.

   b) The article takes the subject too seriously – the writer should 'lighten up'.

   c) The writer chooses examples well.

   d) The writer makes a convincing case.

   e) The writer takes an elitist view (i.e. looking down on ordinary people).

7 Imagine you are a strong supporter of reality TV and the opportunities it gives ordinary people to become famous. Write down three to five good arguments in favour of your case.

8 Look back at Text C. Does this article make being a celebrity seem attractive or unattractive? Back up your answer with three examples from the text.

9 Tabloid newspapers (such as the *Sun*, *Star* and *Daily Mirror*) are often dominated by stories about celebrities. Reality programmes often drive their news coverage. Text C is from a broadsheet newspaper (the *Observer*). How does the writer show that he's not in awe of celebrities but is taking a more detached view?

WATCHING YOU WATCHING ME

The following text is about the way society sometimes keeps close track of people. Text D is from George Orwell's classic novel *Nineteen Eighty-Four* (written in 1948) in which he envisages a world in which people's freedom to be individuals is very limited.

It was a bright cold day in April, and the clocks were striking thirteen. Winston Smith, his chin nuzzled into his breast in an effort to escape the vile wind, slipped quickly through the glass doors of Victory Mansions, though not quickly enough to prevent a swirl of gritty dust from entering along with him.

The hallway smelt of boiled cabbage and old rag mats. At one end of it a coloured poster, too large for indoor display, had been tacked to the wall. It depicted simply an enormous face, more than a metre wide: the face of a man of about forty-five, with a heavy black moustache and ruggedly handsome features. Winston made for the stairs. It was no use trying the lift. Even at the best of times it was seldom working, and at present the electric current was cut off during daylight hours. It was part of the economy drive in preparation for Hate Week. The flat was seven flights up, and Winston, who was thirty-nine, and had a varicose ulcer above his right ankle, went slowly, resting several times on the way. On each landing, opposite the lift shaft, the poster with the enormous face gazed from the wall. It was one of those pictures which are so contrived that the eyes follow you about when you move. BIG BROTHER IS WATCHING YOU, the caption beneath it ran.

Inside the flat a fruity voice was reading out a list of figures which had something to do with the production of pig iron. The voice came from an oblong metal plaque like a dulled mirror which formed part of the surface of the right-hand wall. Winston turned a switch and the voice sank somewhat, though the words were still distinguishable. The instrument (the telescreen, it was called) could be dimmed, but there was no way of shutting it off completely. He moved over to the window: a smallish, frail figure, the meagreness of his body merely emphasized by the blue overalls which were the uniform of the party. His hair was very fair, his face naturally sanguine, his skin roughened by coarse soap and blunt razor blades and the cold of the winter that had just ended.

Outside, even through the shut window-pane, the world looked cold. Down in the street little eddies of wind were whirling dust and torn paper into spirals, and though the sun was shining and the sky a harsh blue, there seemed to be no colour in anything except the posters that were plastered everywhere. The black moustachio'd face gazed down from every commanding corner. There was one on the house front immediately opposite. BIG BROTHER IS WATCHING YOU, the caption said, while the dark eyes looked deep into Winston's own. Down at street level another poster, torn at one corner, flapped fitfully in the wind, alternately covering and uncovering the single word INGSOC. In the far distance a helicopter skimmed down between the roofs, hovered for an instant like a blue-bottle, and darted away again with a curving flight. It was the Police Patrol, snooping into people's windows. The patrols did not matter, however. Only the Thought Police mattered.

Behind Winston's back the voice from the telescreen was still babbling away about pig iron and the overfulfilment of the Ninth Three-Year Plan. The telescreen received and transmitted simultaneously. Any sound that Winston made, above the level of a very low whisper, would be picked up by it; moreover, so long as he remained within the field of vision which the metal plaque commanded, he could be seen as well as heard. There was of course no way of knowing whether you were being watched at any given moment. How often, or on what system, the Thought Police plugged in on any individual wire was guesswork. It was even conceivable that they watched everybody all the time. But at any rate they could plug in your wire whenever they wanted to. You had to live — did live, from habit that became instinct — in the assumption that every sound you made was overheard, and, except in darkness, every movement scrutinized.

Winston kept his back turned to the telescreen. It was safer; though, as he well knew, even a back can be revealing. A kilometre away the Ministry of Truth, his place of work, towered vast and white above the grimy landscape. This, he thought with a sort of vague distaste — this was London, chief city of Airstrip One, itself the third most populous of the provinces of Oceania. He tried to squeeze out some childhood memory that should tell him whether London had always been quite like this. Were there always these vistas of rotting nineteenth-century houses, their sides shored up with baulks of timber, their windows patched with cardboard and their roofs with corrugated iron, their crazy garden walls sagging in all directions? And the bombed sites where the plaster dust swirled in the air and the willow-herb straggled over the heaps of rubble; and the places where the bombs had cleared a larger patch and there had sprung up sordid colonies of wooden dwellings like chicken houses? But it was no use, he could not remember: nothing remained of his childhood except a series of bright-lit tableaux, occurring against no background and mostly unintelligible.

The Ministry of Truth — Minitrue, in Newspeak — was startlingly different from any other object in sight. It was an enormous pyramidal structure of glittering white concrete, soaring up, terrace after terrace, 300 metres into the air. From where Winston stood it was just possible to read, picked out on its white face in elegant lettering, the three slogans of the Party:

WAR IS PEACE

FREEDOM IS SLAVERY

IGNORANCE IS STRENGTH.

ACTIVITIES

1 Look again at Text D. Written in 1948, George Orwell looked ahead to a future world of control and surveillance. How accurate do you think his predictions were? Copy and complete the grid below, filling in the details in the extract which feel like the world today and those which do not.

Details that feel realistic about our society	Details that do not feel realistic

2 The central character in the novel is Winston Smith. Using a spider diagram, record what you learn about him from Text D, which is the opening of the novel.

3 Read the five-word summaries for films and stories below. Then write your own five-word summary for Text D and another book of your choice.

Jolly Green Giant Gets Wed – *Shrek 2*

Big Orange Cat with Attitude – *Garfield* from Sharon Poulton

Amazing Squirrels in Robot Costumes – *I, Robot* from Dalmaine Blignaut

A Dude with Hero Issues – *Spider-Man 2* from Clare Alder

Britain gets a legendary King – *King Arthur* from Maxine Glennerster

From www.capitalfm.com/breakfastshow

CLARA'S DAY

Read 'Clara's Day' (Text E), opposite. It is a complete short story by Penelope Lively. As you read, think about the way Clara behaves, at school and at home, and then look at the clues the writer gives to explain her behaviour.

TEXT E

WHEN CLARA TILLING WAS 15½ she took off all her clothes one morning in school assembly. She walked naked through the lines of girls, past the headmistress and the other staff, and out into the entrance lobby. She had left off her bra and pants already, so all she had to do was unbutton her blouse, remove it and drop it to the floor, and then undo the zipper of her skirt and let that fall. She slipped her feet out of her shoes at the same time and so walked barefoot as well as naked. It all happened very quickly. One or two girls giggled and a sort of rustling noise ran through the assembly hall, like a sudden wind among the trees. The Head hesitated for a moment – she was reading out the tennis team list – and then went on again, firmly. Clara opened the big glass doors and let herself out.

The entrance lobby was empty. The floor was highly polished and she could see her own reflection, a foreshortened pink blur. There was a big bright modern painting on one wall and several comfortable chairs for waiting parents, arranged round an enormous rubber plant and ashtrays on chrome stalks. Clara had sat there herself once, with her mother, waiting for an interview with the Head.

She walked along the corridor to her classroom, which was also quite empty, with thick gold bars of sunlight falling on the desks and a peaceful feeling, as though no one had been here for a long time nor ever would come. Clara opened the cupboard in the corner, took out one of the science overalls and put it on, and then sat down at her desk. After about a minute Mrs Mayhew came in carrying her clothes and her shoes. She said, 'I should put these on now, Clara,' and stood beside her while she did so. 'Would you like to go home?' she asked, and when Clara said that she wouldn't, thank you, Mrs Mayhew went on briskly, 'Right you are, then, Clara. You'd better get on with some homework, then, till the first period.'

All morning people kept coming up to her to say, 'Well done!' or just to pat her on the back. She was a celebrity right up till dinner time but after that it tailed off a bit. Half-way through the morning one of the prefects came in and told her the Head wanted to see her straight after school.

The Head's study was more like a sitting room, except for the big paper-strewn desk that she sat behind. She was busy writing when Clara came in: she just looked up to say, 'Hello, Clara. Sit down. Do you mind if I just finish these reports off? I won't be a minute.' She went on writing and Clara sat and looked at a photo of the Head's husband, who had square sensible-looking glasses, and her three boys who were all the same but different sizes. The Head slapped the pile of reports together and pushed her chair back. 'There ...Well now ... So what was all that about this morning?'

'I don't know,' said Clara.

The Head looked at her, thoughtfully, and Clara looked back. Just before the silence became really embarrassing the Head said, 'I daresay you don't. Were you trying to attract attention?'

Clara considered. 'Well, I would, wouldn't I? Doing a thing like that. I mean — you'd be bound to.'

The Head nodded. 'Quite. Silly question.'

'Oh, no,' said Clara hastily. 'I meant you'd be bound to attract attention. Not be bound to be trying to.'

The Head asked, 'How do you feel about it now?'

Clara tried to examine her feelings, which slithered away like fish. In the end she said, 'I don't really feel anything,' which was, in a way, truthful.

The Head nodded again. 'Everything all right at home?'

'Oh, fine.' Clara assured her. 'Absolutely fine.'

'Good,' said the Head. 'Of course... I was just thinking, there are quite a lot of people in 4B with separated parents, aren't there? Bryony and Susie Tallance and Rachel.'

'And Midge,' said Clara. 'And Lucy Potter.'

'Yes, Five. Six, with you.'

'Twenty-five per cent,' said Clara. 'Just about.'

'Quite. As a matter of fact that's the national average, did you know? One marriage in four.'

'No, I didn't actually,' said Clara.

'Well, it is, I'm afraid. Anyway ...'

'You're not fussing about GCSEs, are you?'

'Not really,' said Clara. 'I mean, I don't like exams, but I don't mind as much as some people.'

'Your mocks were fine,' said the Head. 'Science could have been a bit better. But there shouldn't be any problems there. So ... Are you still going around with Liz Raymond?'

'Mostly,' said Clara. 'And Stephanie.'

'I want people to come and talk to me if there's anything they're worried about,' said the Head. 'Even things that may seem silly. You know. It doesn't have to be large obvious things. Exams and stuff. Anything.'

'Yes,' said Clara.

The phone rang. The Head picked it up and said no, she hadn't, and yes, she'd be along as soon as she could and tell them to wait. She put the receiver down and said, 'It wasn't like you, Clara, was it? I mean — there are a few people one wouldn't be *all* that surprised, if they suddenly did something idiotic or unexpected. But you aren't really like that, are you?'

Clara agreed that she wasn't, really.

'I'll be writing a note to your mother. And if you have an urge to do something like that again come and have a talk to me first, right?' The Head smiled and Clara smiled back. That was all, evidently. Clara got up and left. As she was closing the door she saw the Head looking after her, not smiling now, her expression rather bleak.

Most of the school had gone home but all those in Clara's class who had boyfriends at St. Benet's, which was practically everyone, were hanging around the bus station deliberately not catching buses because St. Benet's came out half an hour later. Clara hung around for a bit too, just to be sociable, and then got on her bus. She sat on the top deck by herself and looked down onto the pavements. It was very hot; everyone young had bare legs, road menders were stripped to the waist, everywhere there was flesh — brown backs and white knees and glimpses of the hair under people's arms and the clefts between breasts and buttocks. In the park, the grass was strewn with sunbathers; there were girls in bikinis sprawled like starfish, face down with a rag of material between their legs and the strings of the top half undone. Clara, with no bra or pants on, could feel warm air washing around between her skin and her clothes. Coming down the stairs as the bus approached her stop, she had to hold down her skirt in case it blew up.

Her mother was already home. She worked part-time as a dentist's receptionist and had what were called flexible hours, which meant more or less that she worked when it suited her. Afternoons, nowadays, often didn't suit because Stan, her friend, who was an actor, was only free in the afternoons.

Stan wasn't there today though. Clara came into the kitchen where her mother was drinking tea and looking at a magazine. 'Hi!' she said. 'Any news?' which was what she said most days. Clara said that there was no news and her mother went on reading. Presently she yawned, pushed the magazine over to Clara and went upstairs to have a bath. Clara had another cup of tea and leafed through the magazine and then began to do her homework.

The Head's letter came a couple of days later. Clara heard the post flop onto the doormat and when she looked over the bannister she knew at once what the typed envelope must be. At the same moment Stan, who had stayed the night, came out of her mother's room on his way to the bathroom. He wore underpants and had a towel slung around his neck like a football scarf, and was humming to himself. When he saw her he said, 'Wotcha! How's tricks, then?' and Clara pulled her dressing gown more closely round her and said, 'Fine thanks.'

'That's the stuff,' said Stan vaguely. 'Hey – I got a couple of tickets for the show. Bring a friend, OK?' He was a stocky muscular man with a lot of black hair on his chest. The smell of him, across the landing, was powerful – a huge inescapable wave of man smell: sweat and aftershave and something you could not put your finger on. Clara always knew when he was in the house before she opened the sitting room door because whiffs of him gusted about the place. She said, 'Thanks very much. That would be super,' and edged into her room.

When she came down they were both having breakfast. Her mother was just opening the post. She said, 'Coffee on the stove, lovey. Oh goody – my tax rebate's come.' She opened the Head's letter and began to read. First she stared at it with a puzzled look and then she began to laugh. She clapped her hand over her mouth, spluttering. 'I don't believe it!' she cried. 'Clara, I simply do not believe it! Stan just listen to this … isn't she the most incredible girl! Guess what she did! She took off all her clothes in school assembly and walked out starkers!' She handed the letter to Stan and went on laughing.

Stan read the letter. Grinning hugely, he looked up at Clara. 'She'll have done it for a dare, I bet. Good on

yer, Clara. Terrific! God, I wish I'd been there!' He patted Clara's arm and Clara froze. She went completely rigid, as though she had turned to cement, and when eventually she moved a leg it seemed as though it should make a cracking noise.

Her mother had stopped laughing and was talking again. '… the last thing anyone would have expected of you, lovey. You've always been such a prude. Ever since you were a toddler. Talk about modest! Honestly, Stan, she was hilarious, as a little kid – I can see her now, sitting on the beach at Camber clutching a towel round her in case anyone got a glimpse of her bum when she was changing. Aged 10. And when her bust grew she used to sit hunched over like a spoon so no one would notice it. And if she had to strip off for the doctor you'd have thought that he'd been about to rape her, from her expression. Even now I can't get her out of that Victorian one-piece school regulation bathing costume – and it's not as though she's not got a good shape. 'Smashing!' said Stan, slurping his coffee.

'…spot of puppy fat still but that's going, good hips, my legs if I may say so. Which is what makes this such an absolute scream. Honestly, sweetie, I wouldn't have thought you had it in you. I mean, I've not been allowed to see her in the buff myself since she was 12. Honestly, I've wondered once or twice if there was something wrong with the girl.' Her mother beamed across the breakfast table. 'Anyway, old Mrs Whatsit doesn't seem to be making a fuss. She just thinks I ought to know. More coffee, anyone? God, look at the time! And I said I'd be in early today … I'm off. Leave the breakfast things, lovey – we'll do them later. Coming, Stan?'

Clara went on sitting at the table. She ate a piece of toast and drank her coffee. Her mother and Stan bustled about collecting her purse and his jacket and banged out of the house, shouting goodbye. The front gate clicked, the car door slammed, and then Clara began to cry, the tears dripping from her chin onto her folded arms and her face screwed up like a small child's.

1   With a partner, discuss what happens in the story by responding to these questions:

a) How can we tell from the first paragraph that Clara has planned this incident in advance?

b) Look at the Head's reaction to Clara's behaviour, in the assembly, and later in her office.
    ✦ Think of a word to describe the Head's response.
    ✦ Why do you think she reacted like this?

c) In the paragraph at the top of page 76 (on the right), the Head answers the telephone. Although we are not told what the person on the other end says, we can infer it. See if you can guess what is said in these gaps:

Caller	Headteacher
	No, she hadn't
	Yes, she'd be along as soon as she could and tell them to wait

d) We can tell from the Head's response that she thinks she knows why

d) We can all tell from the Head's response that she thinks she knows why Clara undressed. What clues are there about the Head's thoughts?

2   Explore the different characters by copying and completing this grid.

What we learn from the story about …	Clara	Clara's mother	Stan
Appearance			
The way they speak			
Their relationship with each other			
Any other comments about the character			

3   Writers use a number of techniques to make us feel sympathetic or unsympathetic towards characters. For example, in this story we are intended to like Clara and feel unsympathetic to Stan.

a) Write down three ways that the writer makes us feel sympathetic towards Clara.

b) Write down three ways that the writer makes us feel unsympathetic towards Stan.

UNIT CHALLENGES

1. Debate

Prepare a speech for a debate on one of the topics opposite. You can argue either for or against the motion. Your speech should last three minutes and, although you can use some brief notes, you are expected to make eye-contact with the audience, address them directly, and use body language in a way that shows you are being spontaneous and not simply prepared.

Topics:
+ Reality television shows have gone too far.
+ Students should be given more freedom in school.
+ Fashion doesn't increase a person's individuality; it reduces it.

(HINTS)
+ Structure your argument around two or three main ideas.
+ Make it easy for your listeners to follow the direction of your argument using phrases such as: 'I will make three main points … This is my first main point … my second main point is …'.
+ Use standard English.
+ Concentrate on standing still, using minimal notes, looking at your audience, involving all of them as you speak (i.e. don't just look in one direction).

2. Personal response

Write a personal response to the story, 'Clara's Day'. Use the following headings to structure your response (although you don't have to write down the subheadings in your essay):
+ What the story is about
+ The character of Clara
+ Her relationships at home
+ What you think the 'message' of the story is
+ Your overall response to the story – what you like/what you don't like

(HINTS)
+ Write in an impersonal style until the final paragraph. This means generally avoiding using the pronouns 'I' and 'me'. Instead, say 'the story is about …', 'Clara shows that she …'.
+ Rather than using subheadings, use topic sentences at the start of paragraphs to show your reader what the main subject is, like this: 'Clara's relationships at home seem more complicated than …'.
+ Use connectives to link ideas and show the direction of your writing. Useful connectives include: however, although, despite this, later, meanwhile, therefore.
+ Make comments on the language used in the text. Embed short quotations into your own sentences, like this: 'The writer hints at the distance that exists between Clara and Stan. For example, when he is drinking his coffee, the writer uses the verb 'slurping'. This suggests that …'.

✦ Use your final paragraph to write more personally, like this: 'Overall I enjoyed the story. I was interested by …'.

3. Characterization

Explore the way writers can present characters as sympathetic or unsympathetic. Below is the outline of a character. Your challenge is to write two story openings – one designed to make us like your chosen character; the other designed to make us unsympathetic towards her or him. Use the steps below to guide you.

a) Build a character
   Name:
   Age:
   Interests:
   Main physical features (hair colour, height, dress sense, and so on):

b) Now choose an opening sequence:
   ✦ Option A – Your character is on holiday and notices strange behaviour.
   ✦ Option B – Your character is heading home after seeing friends and starts to think that he or she is being followed.
   ✦ Option C – Your character is in a supermarket and realizes that members of staff are eyeing her or him suspiciously.

HINTS

As you write, think about what effect the following choices will have on your text:
✦ use of first name/no name
✦ type of relationships with other people
✦ insight/ignorance of your character's feelings
✦ positive/negative vocabulary.

To make a character sympathetic, try:	To make a character unsympathetic, try:
Using her/his first name, e.g. *Charles stood at the edge of the car park …*	Using her/his surname, or not using a name, e.g. *Brinkley stood at the edge of the car park …*
Showing positive relationships/conversations with other people, e.g. *'Oh hi there,' Charles said when he saw Danni …*	Showing other people taking a negative view of your character, e.g. *'Just watch him, that's all,' said Sarah as Brinkley came back into the room …*
Showing us your character's point of view so that we feel we know what she/he is like, e.g. *Charles couldn't wait till the day was over. He looked at …*	Not giving much insight into the character's inner feelings.
Using positive vocabulary about your character.	Using negative associations – instead of *Brinkley walked* say *Brinkley shuffled … sloped in … drifted …*

ASSESS YOUR LEARNING

- Adapt your talk to different contexts with increasing confidence
- Engage your listener with a variety of expressions and vocabulary
- Use standard English with fluency

You should be gaining confidence with talking in various situations.

a) Look at the situations listed below. For each one, give yourself a 'confidence rating' * to *****.

Solo prepared talk	Solo unprepared talk (e.g. spontaneous debate)	1:1 paired discussion	Making a comment in a small group	Role-playing a character	Scripted drama work

b) Which areas are weakest? Think about the kind of activities that would target the areas you need more practice in.

- Identify different layers of meaning and comment on their significance and effect
- Give a personal and critical response to thematic, structural and linguistic features in literature

This unit has presented you with some meaty, challenging texts. It has encouraged you to look beneath the surface to see how writers create meaning by implication (hints).

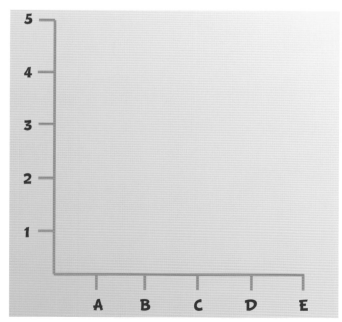

Thinking about your response either to *Nineteen Eighty-Four* or 'Clara's Day', evaluate the way your reading is developing. Draw up a bar chart to show the way you are developing each aspect of your reading skills.

a) Put A to E along the X axis and 1 to 5 along the Y axis.

b) Use the Y axis to indicate strength/weakness for each area. The strongest level should be marked 5.

The labels A to E represent:

A: Understanding what happens in a story or non-fiction text

B: Noticing features about characters – even when they are implied rather than directly stated

C: Being able to comment on the way a story is structured

D: Noticing what the key themes in a text are

E: Commenting on the language used

- Write confidently showing appropriate choices of style in a range of forms
- Develop characters and settings in narrative writing

a) You should be developing your skills in writing in a range of styles. Use the list below to find a way of presenting visually the areas you are strongest and weakest in, and those that you need more practice in.

Leaflets, fact-sheets, posters, websites, advertisements, scripts, stories, poems, speeches, autobiography, opinion pieces, news articles

b) Look at the aspects of narrative writing, listed below:

- structuring stories
- building a character
- establishing setting.

Jot down three areas beside each aspect, in which you feel your skills are developing. For example, you might feel you are improving your story openings, the build up of tension and their resolution.

FINISHING LINE

Think of a caption for this cartoon, or think who the people are and why they have chosen to sunbathe here.

Learning objectives

By the end of this unit you should be able to:

- Make a significant contribution to discussion, including evaluating others' ideas
- Use vocabulary precisely and organize your talk to communicate clearly

- Show understanding of ways in which meaning and information are conveyed in a range of texts

- Write confidently, showing appropriate choices of style in a range of forms
- Use paragraphing and punctuation to make sequence of ideas clear

INTRODUCTION

One of the features that makes humans different from animals is our ability to laugh. This unit is all about humour. It looks at different types of humour, expressed in different forms, such as jokes, playscripts, poems, a monologue and a novel.

(WARM-UP)

I Here are five jokes from the website www.comedycentral.com. With a partner or in a small group, discuss:
- ✦ which is funniest and which is least funny
- ✦ what you can say about the type of humour each joke uses (e.g. word play, absurdity, surprise).

1
TWO GOLDFISH WERE IN THEIR TANK. ONE TURNS TO THE OTHER AND SAYS, 'YOU MAN THE GUNS, I'LL DRIVE.'

2
Q: WHAT WEIGHS 2,000 POUNDS AND PINCHES?
A: AN ELEPHANT WEARING A TIGHT TUXEDO!

3
Q: WHAT DO ALEXANDER THE GREAT AND KERMIT THE FROG HAVE IN COMMON?
A: THEIR MIDDLE NAME.

4
Q: WHAT DID THE APPLE SAY TO THE WORM?
A: YOU'RE BORING ME.

5
Q: WHY DID THE RAM FALL OFF THE CLIFF?
A: BECAUSE HE DIDN'T SEE THE EWE TURN.

2 Here are four comments people have made about humour. Read them and talk about:

+ which you like
+ which you agree with most.

> Humour can be dissected as a frog can, but the thing dies in the process and the innards are discouraging to any but the pure scientific mind.
> *E.B. White*

> Defining and analysing humour is a pastime of humourless people.
> *Robert Benchley*

> Humour is by far the most significant activity of the human brain.
> *Edward De Bono*

> A sense of humour is part of the art of leadership, of getting along with people, of getting things done.
> *Dwight D. Eisenhower*

COMEDY SCRIPTS

This section looks at a collection of comedy scripts – a sketch, a movie script and a monologue. They are very different in their written style and humour. They should help you to think about the way comedy is created on stage, screen and page.

These extracts are best read aloud, but before you do this, think carefully about the part you have been given. How might you present your character through the way that you read their part? Think about the pace, intonation, accent, and use of pauses in your speech.

During the readings aloud, listen carefully to everyone's speeches. Consider how each participant (including yourself) could improve his or her delivery.

This sketch is taken from the classic television comedy show, *Monty Python's Flying Circus*.

The Man Who Speaks in Anagrams

Palin: Our next guest is a man who speaks entirely in anagrams.
Idle: That si creeoct.
Palin: Do you enjoy it?
Idle: I stom certainly od. Revy chum so.
Palin: And what's your name?

Idle: Hamrag – Hamrag Yatlerot.

Palin: Well, Graham, nice to have you on the show. Now, where do you come from?

Idle: Bumcreland.

Palin: Cumberland?

Idle: Staht sit sepricly.

Palin: And I believe you're working on an anagram version of Shakespeare?

Idle: Sey, Sey – taht si crreoct, er – ta the mnemot I'm wroking on *The Mating of the Wersh*.

Palin: *The Mating of the Wersh*? By William Shakespeare?

Idle: Nay, bu Malliwi Rapesheake.

Palin: And what else?

Idle: *Two Netlemeg of Verona, Twelfth Thing, The Chamrent of Venice* …

Palin: Have you done *Hamlet*?

Idle: Thamle. 'Be ot or bot neo t, taht is the nestqui.'

Palin: And what is your next project?

Idle: *Ring Kichard the Thrid*.

Palin: I'm sorry?

Idle: 'A shroe! A shroe! My dingkome for a shroe!'

Palin: Ah, Ring Kichard, yes but surely that's not an anagram, that's a spoonerism.

Idle: If you're going to split hairs I'm going to go.

YOU'LL NEVER CATCH ME, COPPER!

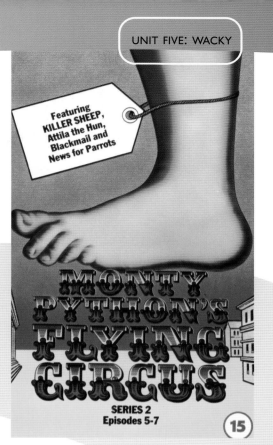

Featuring KILLER SHEEP, Attila the Hun, Blackmail and News for Parrots

MONTY PYTHON'S FLYING CIRCUS

SERIES 2
Episodes 5-7

(15)

HE'S MAKING HIS GETTA'WAY IN A PRAM. QUICK, AFTER HIM.

Glossary:

spoonerism – words or phrases in which letters or syllables get swapped. This often happens accidentally in slips of the tongue (or 'tips of the slung' as spoonerisms are often affectionately called!)

85

This is an extract from the screenplay of *Austin Powers: International Man of Mystery*. In it Dr Evil is threatening to blow up the world.

Dr Evil and Number Two watch a large screen. We see stock footage of a Russian warhead. We cut into a close-up of RUSSIAN SOLDIERS being taken prisoner by VIRTUCON SOLDIERS in the front of a military vehicle.

Dr Evil: Gentlemen, Phase One is complete. The warhead is ours. Let Phase Two begin! Patch us through to the United Nations security secret meeting room.

INTERNATIONAL UN SECRET MEETING ROOM

REPRESENTATIVES of various countries in their traditional garb around a large UN-style meeting table. The BRITISH are dressed in bowler hats. The AMERICANS all look like JFK. The CANADIANS are dressed as Mounties. The ARABS are dressed in ceremonial robes, etc.

Dr Evil: Gentlemen, my name is Dr Evil.

They all look up at the SCREEN.

Dr Evil: In a little while, you'll find out that the Kreplachistani warhead has gone missing. Well, it's in safe hands. If you want it back, you'll have to pay me ... ONE MILLION DOLLARS!

The UN representatives are confused.
Number Two COUGHS.

Dr Evil: (frustrated) Sorry. ONE-HUNDRED BILLION DOLLARS!

The representatives ARGUE amongst themselves.

United Nations Secretary: Gentlemen, silence! (to Dr Evil) Now, Mr Evil ...

Dr Evil: (angry) Doctor Evil! I didn't spend six years in evil medical school to be called 'mister'.

United Nations Secretary: Excuse me. Dr Evil, it is the policy of the United Nations not to negotiate with terrorists.

Dr Evil: Fine, have it your way. Gentlemen, you have five days to come up with one-hundred billion dollars. If you fail to do so, we'll set off the warhead and destroy the world.

United Nations Secretary: You can't destroy the world with a single warhead.

Dr Evil: Really? So long.

The screen goes BLANK.

Dr Evil: (to evil associates) Gentlemen, in exactly five days from now, we will be one-hundred billion dollars richer. (laughing) Ha-ha-ha-ha. (slightly louder) Ha-ha-ha-ha.

Evil Associates: (laughing with him) Ha-ha-ha-ha.

Dr Evil & ASSOCIATES: (louder and more staccato) HA-HA-HA-HA-HA!(louder again, and even more evil and maniacal) HA-HA-HA-HA-HA-HA-HA-HA! (pause) Ohhhh, ahhhhhh ... (pause, quieter) Ohhh, hmmmm. (pause, very quiet) hmn.

There is an uncomfortable pause, because clearly we should have FADED TO BLACK. The Evil Associates look around the room, not knowing what to do with themselves.

Dr Evil: Okay ... Well ... I think I'm going to watch some TV.

Evil Associates: Okay. Sure.

They exit the frame awkwardly.

A monologue is a play spoken by one character. Writer Alan Bennett has written a series of television monologues, each lasting half an hour. This is the opening of *A Chip in the Sugar* in which, for the BBC Production, Alan Bennett himself played the role of Graham.

Graham is a mild middle-aged man. The play is set in his bedroom, a small room with one window and one door. It is furnished with a single bed, a wardrobe, two chairs and nothing much else.

I'd just taken her tea up this morning when she said, 'Graham, I think the world of you.' I said, 'I think the world of you.' And she said, 'That's all right then.' I said, 'What's brought this on?' She said, 'Nothing. This tea looks strong, pull the curtains.' Of course I knew what had brought it on. She said, 'I wouldn't like you to think you're not Number One.' So I said, 'Well, you're Number One with me too. Give me your teeth. I'll swill them.'

What it was we'd had a spot of excitement yesterday: we ran into a bit of Mother's past. I said to her, ' I didn't know you had a past. I thought I was your past.' She said, 'You?' I said, 'Well, we go back a long way. How does he fit in vis-à-vis Dad?' She laughed. 'Oh, he was pre-Dad.' I said, 'Pre-Dad? I'm surprised you remember him, you don't remember to switch your blanket off.' She said, 'That's different. His name's Turnbull.' I said, 'I know. He said.'

I'd parked her by the war memorial on her usual seat while I went and got some reading matter. Then I waited while she went and spent a penny in the disabled toilet. She's not actually disabled, her memory's bad, but she says she prefers their toilets because you get more elbow room. She always takes forever, diddling her hands and what not, and when she eventually comes back it turns out she's been chatting to the attendant. I said, 'What about?' She said, 'Hanging. She was in favour of stiffer penalties for minor offences and I thought, "Well, we know better, our Graham and me." I wish you'd been there, love; you could have given her the statistics, where are we going for our tea?'

The thing about Mam is that though she's never had a proper education, she's picked up enough from me to be able to hold her own discussions about up-to-the-minute issues like the environment and the colour problem, and for a woman of her age and background she has a very liberal slant. She'll look at my *Guardian* and she actually thinks for herself. Doctor Chaudhury said to me, 'Full marks, Graham. The best way to avoid a broken hip is to have a flexible mind. Keep up the good work.'

They go mad round the war memorial so when we cross over I'll generally slip my arm through hers until we're safely across, only once we're on the pavement she'll postpone letting go, because once upon a time we got stopped by one of these questionnaire women who reckons to take us for husband and wife. I mean, Mam's got white hair. She was doing this dodge and I said, 'Mam, let go of my arm.' I didn't really wrench it, only next thing I knew she's flat on the pavement. I said, 'Oh my God, Mother.'

People gather round and I pick up her bag and she sits up and says, 'I've laddered both my stockings,' I said, 'Never mind your stockings, what about your pelvis?' She says, 'It's these bifocals. They tell you not to look down. I was avoiding some sick.' Somebody says, 'That's a familiar voice,' and there's a little fellow bending over her, green trilby hat, shorty raincoat. 'Hello,' he says, 'remember me?'

Well, she doesn't remember people, I know for a fact because she swore me down she'd never met Joy Buckle, who teaches Flowers in Felt and Fabric at my day care centre. I said, 'You have met Joy, you knitted her a tea cosy.' That's all she can knit, tea cosies. And bed socks. Both outmoded articles. I said to her, 'Branch out. If you can knit tea cosies you can knit skiing hats.' She says, 'Well, I will.' Only I have to stand over her or else she'll still leave a hole for the spout. 'Anyway,' I said, 'you do remember Joy because you said she had some shocking eyebrows.' She said, 'I hope you didn't tell her that.' I said, 'Of course I didn't.' She said, 'Well, I don't remember.' And that's the way she is, she doesn't remember and here's this little fellow saying, 'Do you remember me?' So I said, 'No she won't. Come on, Mother. Let's get you up.' Only she says, 'Remember you? Of course. It's Frank Turnbull. It must be fifty tears.' He said 'Fifty-two. Filey. 1934.' She said, 'Sea-Crest.' He said, 'No sand in the bedrooms.' And they both cracked out laughing.

Meanwhile she's still stuck on the cold pavement. I said, 'Come along, Mother. We don't want piles.' Only he butts in again. He says, 'With respect, it's advisable not to move a person until it's been ascertained no bones are broken. I was in the St John's Ambulance Brigade.' 'Yes,' said Mother, 'and who did you learn the bandaging on?' And they both burst our laughing again. He had on these bright yellow gloves, could have been a bookie.

Eventually, I get my arms round her waist and hoist her up, only his lordship's no help as he claims to have a bad back. When I've finally got her restored to the perpendicular she introduces him. 'This is Frank Turnbull, a friend of mine from the old days.' What old days? First time I knew there were any old days.

ACTIVITIES

1 Give feedback to the performers of each script or, if you were one of the performers, listen to the feedback. It should be focused on how the characters were brought to life, referring to issues such as:
- ✦ pace
- ✦ intonation
- ✦ accent
- ✦ use of pauses.

2 Look again at Text A.
 a) What do you like about it?
 b) Which parts did you find particularly funny?
 c) Did any of it not work for you?
 d) Think of a similar verbal game as the starting point for a sketch, such as:
  ✦ the woman who talks in rhyme
  ✦ the man who says words backwards.
  Write the opening sequence of the sketch.

3 Look at the list of types of comedy, below. Which of these do you think we find in Text B?

Type of comedy	Definition
Wit	This is intellectual comedy that uses quick-fire word-play and clever jokes.
Romantic comedy	This usually focuses on a pair of lovers and their struggle to find romance. It may involve some extraordinary circumstances, e.g. magic, dream.
Satire	This type of comedy has a critical purpose. The aim is not to make people 'laugh with' the characters but 'laugh at' them, exposing people's stupidity or other vices. It is often used to comment on political situations and topical issues.
Parody	This is a more gentle form of comedy – it copies the style of people and genres, making fun of them. The film *Airplane* is a good example: it is a spoof of other films.
Farce	This is all about hearty laughter. It presents highly exaggerated and caricatured characters and often has an unlikely plot.

4 The Austin Powers movies often divide viewers' opinions. Some people love their fast-paced comedy. Other people find them rude and childish.

a) Read the review from the *Radio Times* in Text D.

TEXT D

"Yeah, baby!"

Radio Times Rating | ★★★★

Director | **Jay Roach**
Starring | **Mike Myers & Elizabeth Hurley**
Running Time | **90mins**
Country of Origin | **US**

This Swinging Sixties spy spoof is a fast, furious and fabulously funny ride that expertly mocks every groovy fad, psychedelic fashion and musical style of the period. Mike Myers is brilliant as the secret agent-cum-fashion photographer, cryogenically frozen so he can foil the world domination plans of his arch nemesis Dr Evil (Myers again) in the 1990s. Witty, sophisticated and hysterically stupid by turns, the side-splitting humour arises from clever culture-clash comedy (free love versus safe sex), knockabout farce, Austin's catch phrases — "Oh, behave!" — and countless references to 007, Matt Helm and *Our Man Flint*. Even Elizabeth Hurley is fantastic as ersatz Bond girl Vanessa Kensington. **AJ**

b) Think what a critic who loathes the film might say. Write the first few sentences of a really negative movie review. You could start like this: 'There are few genuine laughs here …'

5 Look back at Text C.

a) Talk about what we learn about the character of Graham and his relationship with his mother.
Consider:
- ✦ the way he speaks
- ✦ what we learn about his background
- ✦ what he and his mother say to each other
- ✦ who cares for whom.

b) Record your understanding of Graham, using a spider diagram.

6 Although Text C is a comedy, it has a very different style from the other texts. In what ways do you think it is humorous?

7 Take the character below and write the opening of a monologue which illuminates her or his character:

Name:	Alex Tait (you decide whether female or male)
Age:	27
Set-up:	Since childhood, Alex has wanted to be an actor. Despite completing drama school, s/he has had little real work, apart from minor roles in a local pantomime and occasional jobs promoting new products at trade fairs. But s/he is still certain that the big time – in television or movies – lies just ahead. Most people think that s/he has no chance.

SPOOF!

This section explores literary parody. The poet W.H. Auden said that if he was teaching English (which he did, briefly) he would teach it through parody, because it was the best way of 'getting inside' a writer's style.

 Read poems E to I. They are all parodies of traditional nursery rhymes, written in the style of famous poets. Think about which nursery rhymes they parody.

 **TEXT E**

Written in the style of
William Shakespeare

Sweet coz, how contrary thy garden grows,
We have heard, and fain would learn the manner o't.

MARY
My liege, I may not speak with feigning lips
To say that this my garden is as those,
Which custom and dull usage have made stale
And hackneyed in the world's regard. For they
In flowers, shrubs, and bosky coppices
Abound, and arbours green-embowered.
But my poor plot teems with those tiny shells,
Which, clinging to the adamantine cliffs,
Beat back the envious ocean's boist'rous surge
In strong despite. And, when mild zephyrs breathe,
Sweet silvern bells hard by make melody.
And, in the stead of flowers, row on row
Of stateliest damsels, each one perfect bloom,
Make bright my borders. So my garden grows,
More stranger none.

We do believe it well.

G.F. Forrest

TEXT F

Written in the style of
William Wordsworth

Close by the cataract a widow dwelt
With but a son and daughter to beguile
Her failing years; her lad was christened Jack,
His sister, Jill. Once, in a time of drought,
Their well being dry, she sent her young ones off,
Bearing a bucket, to a wholesome tarn
High on the hill, to fetch some water home.
Descending, Jack, missing the sheep track, tripped
And in his headlong fall injured his pate;
His sister likewise tumbled after him.
With all convenient speed Jack trotted home,
Repaired his skull with rustic remedy,
Paper and vinegar – at which Jill scoffed
Invoking thus her beldam's violent rage.

Gerard Benson

Written in the style of
Ernest Hemingway

'Come in, Jack.'
'I d'wanta come in.'
'D'wanta come in, hell. Come in bright boy.'
They went in.
'I'll have eats now,' she said. She was fat and red.
'I d'want nothing,' Jack said. He was thin and pale.
'D'want nothin' hell. You have eats now, bright boy.'
She called the waiter. 'Bud,' she said, 'gimmie bacon and beans – twice.'
Bud brought the bacon and beans.
'I d'want bacon. It's too fat,' said Jack.
'D'want bacon, hell. I'll eat the fat. You eat the lean. OK, big boy?'
'OK,' Jack said.
They had eats.
'Now lick the plate clean,' she said.
'Aw, honey,' said Jack, 'I aint gotta, do I?
'Yup,' she said. 'You gotta.'
They both licked their plates clean.

Henry Hetherington

Written in the style of
Lord Macaulay

Then up rose Gorgius Porgius
Of pudding and of pie –
So stands it in the nursery book,
To witness if I lie –
He marked the maidens' coming;
Of no avail their tears;
He kissed them all both large and small,
At least so it appears.

So there he stood triumphant,
That wrought the deed of shame,
Thinking, no doubt, when they came out,
He might repeat the game.
But, when the maidens later
Came trooping forth to play,
'Twas then our hero's courage failed,
His previous boldness naught availed,
Before the advancing host he quailed,
And turned, and fled away.

G.F. Forrest

Written in the style of
Alexander Pope

O undulate, thou innocent, and rest
Upon this arboraceous summit's breast.
When that the zephyrs rouse themselves irate,
Thy nest shall with like fervour oscillate;
And, when the branch by sudden blast be riven,
May watching cherubs waft thy soul to heaven.

Rhoda Tuck Pook

ACTIVITIES

1   Working with a partner or in a small group, complete the grid below. First, decide which nursery rhyme is being parodied. Then, using the style checklist, work out what you can about the style of the writers who are being parodied.

Text	What the nursery rhyme is	What you can work out about the style of the writer
E		
F		
G		
H		
I		

Style checklist

+ Does the tone feel formal/informal?
+ Is the vocabulary complex/simple?
+ Is the subject matter abstract/concrete?
+ Is the style verbose (wordy), stark, descriptive, alliterative (repeating initial letters), highly structured, rhyming, blank verse (poetry that doesn't rhyme)?

2   Which parody do you like most and why?

3   Now try to write your own parody – of a news report on TV. Use the nursery rhyme of Humpty Dumpty and write the opening of the report. You might start like this:

You join me live in Toytown where there is a real sense of panic and disbelief. Unconfirmed reports are saying that Humpty Dumpty has fallen from his wall …

RIDICULING RIDICULE

 The writer David Sedaris remembers the days in school when he was made to feel foolish because of a speech impediment (he spoke with a lisp). Some writers would recount this sort of recollection in a serious style, emphasizing the humiliation and the bullying attitude of Miss Samson. As you read Text J, think about how and why David Sedaris uses humour to bring his memory alive.

TEXT J

Go Carolina

Anyone who watches even the slightest amount of TV is familiar with the scene: An agent knocks on the door of some seemingly ordinary home or office. The door opens, and the person holding the knob is asked to identify himself. The agent then says, "I'm going to ask you to come with me."

They're always remarkably calm, these agents. If asked "Why do I need to go anywhere with you?" they'll straighten their cuffs or idly brush stray hairs from the sleeves of their sport coats and say, "Oh, I think we both know why."

The suspect then chooses between doing things the hard way and doing things the easy way, and the scene ends with either gunfire or the gentlemanly application of handcuffs. Occasionally it's a case of mistaken identity, but most often the suspect knows exactly why he's being taken. It seems he's been expecting this to happen. The anticipation has ruled his life, and now, finally, the wait is over. You're sometimes led to believe that this person is actually relieved, but I've never bought it. Though it probably has its moments, the average day spent in hiding is bound to beat the average day spent in prison. When it comes time to decide who gets the bottom bunk, I think anyone would agree that there's a lot to be said for doing things the hard way.

The agent came for me during a geography lesson. She entered the room and nodded at my fifth-grade teacher, who stood frowning at a map of Europe.

What would needle me later was the realization that this had all been prearranged. My capture had been scheduled to go down at exactly 2:30 on a Thursday afternoon. The agent would be wearing a dung-colored blazer over a red knit turtleneck, her heels sensibly low in case the suspect should attempt a quick getaway.

"David," the teacher said, "this is Miss Samson, and she'd like you to go with her now."

No one else had been called. So why me? I ran down a list of recent crimes, looking for a conviction

that might stick. Setting fire to a reportedly flameproof Halloween costume, stealing a set of barbecue tongs from an unguarded patio, altering the word *hit* on a list of rules posted on the gymnasium door; never did it occur to me that I might be innocent.

"You might want to take your books with you," the teacher said. "And your jacket. You probably won't be back before the bell rings."

Though she seemed old at the time, the agent was most likely fresh out of college. She walked beside me and asked what appeared to be an innocent and unrelated question: "So, which do you like better, State or Carolina?"

She was referring to the athletic rivalry between the Triangle area's two largest universities. Those who cared about such things tended to express their allegiance by wearing either Tar Heel powder blue, or Wolf Pack red, two colors that managed to look good on no one. The question of team preference was common in our part of North Carolina, and the answer supposedly spoke volumes about the kind of person you either were or hoped to become. I had no interest in football or basketball but had learned it was best to pretend otherwise. If a boy didn't care for barbecued chicken or potato chips, people would accept it as a matter of personal taste, saying, "Oh well, I guess it takes all kinds." You could turn up your nose at the president or Coke or even God, but there were names for boys who didn't like sports. When the subject came up, I found it best to ask which team my questioner preferred. Then I'd say, "Really? Me, too!"

Asked by the agent which team I supported, I took my cue from her turtleneck and told her that I was for State. "Definitely State. State all the way."

It was an answer I would regret for years to come.

"State, did you say?" the agent asked.

"Yes, State. They're the greatest."

"I see." She led me through an unmarked door near the principal's office, into a small, windowless room furnished with two facing desks. It was the kind where you'd grill someone until they snapped, the kind

frequently painted so as to cover the bloodstains. She gestured toward what was to become my regular seat, then continued her line of questioning.

"And what exactly are they, State and Carolina?"

"Colleges? Universities?"

She opened a file on her desk, saying "Yes, you're right. Your answers are correct, but you're saying them incorrectly. You're telling me that they're college*th* and univer*thitieth*, when actually they're college*s* and universitie*s*. You're giving me a *th* sound instead of a nice clear *s*. Can you hear the distinction between the two different sound*s*?"

I nodded.

"May I please have an actual an*s*wer?"

"Uh-huh."

" 'Uh-huh' i*s* not a word."

"Okay."

"Okay what?"

"Okay," I said. "Sure, I can hear it."

"You can hear what, the di*s*tinction? The contra*s*t?"

"Yeah, that."

It was the first battle of my war against the letter *s*, and I was determined to dig my foxhole before the sun went down. According to Agent Samson, a "*s*tate certified *s*peech therapi*s*t," my *s* was sibilate, meaning that I lisped. This was not news to me.

"Our goal i*s* to work together until eventually you can *s*peak correctly," Agent Samson said. She made a great show of enunciating her own sparkling *s*'s, and the effect was profoundly irritating. "I'm trying to help you, but the longer you play the*s*e little game*s* the longer thi*s* i*s* going to take."

The woman spoke with a heavy western North Carolina accent, which I used to discredit her authority. Here was a person for whom the word *pen* had two syllables. Her people undoubtedly drank from clay jugs and hollered for Paw when the vittles were ready — so who was she to advise me on anything? Over the coming years I found a crack in each of the therapists sent to train what Miss Samson now defined as my lazy tongue. "That'*s* its problem," she said. "It'*s* just plain lazy."

ACTIVITIES

1   What impression do you get of the writer then (as a child) and now (as an adult looking back?

2   Look at the quirky way David Sedaris starts his story. Many writers might have used a more conventional (predictable) opening paragraph. Write a more straightforward opening. Then compare it with the impact of his opening paragraph.

3   Focus on the character of Miss Samson.
    a) How does the writer make her seem menacing and unpleasant?
    b) What do you think the writer means when he says that he used her heavy western North Carolina accent 'to discredit her authority'?
    c) If you were casting someone to play this part in a TV or film version of the story:
       ✦ who would you choose?
       ✦ what should the actor look, speak and behave like?
    Write a summary of the casting notes you would give.

4   Think about the humour in this extract.
    a) What do you find funny?
    b) How does the writer's style make an unpleasant situation comical?
    c) Why do you think David Sedaris chose to make this recount humorous? (Think carefully about the beneficial effects of humour.)

UNIT CHALLENGES

1. Discussion

In 2004, the BBC held a viewers' poll to decide on 'Britain's Best Sitcom'. These were the top ten nominations:

BLACKADDER   ONLY FOOLS AND HORSES

VICAR OF DIBLEY   DAD'S ARMY

FAWLTY TOWERS   YES MINISTER

PORRIDGE   OPEN ALL HOURS

THE GOOD LIFE   ONE FOOT IN THE GRAVE

Discuss which sitcom is best – you may wish to turn it into a formal debate.

Think about how you will organize the discussion:
+ Should one person be the Chair?
+ What is the role of the Chair?
+ How will the Chair make sure that everyone contributes?
+ How will you make the case for each choice?
+ Will everyone in the group be given a certain amount of time to put forward an idea, or will your discussion be more fluid and unstructured?
+ How will the winner be decided?

Aim to make a full contribution to the discussion, putting your case as clearly and forcefully as possible. Ask other members of the class to serve as observers and to give you individual and group feedback on how you perform.

2. Personal writing

Choose a memory that has had a powerful effect upon you, like David Sedaris's recollection of his speech lessons. Write about it in a way that brings the memory powerfully to life, giving details about places, people, sounds and smells. Use humour if you wish. Include dialogue to recreate what was said at the time.

You might choose a memory such as:
+ getting into trouble at school or home
+ making a fool of yourself
+ a moment of danger.

3. Comic writing

Write a comic script or story opening based on a nursery rhyme. You could try a modern updated version, as Roald Dahl does in his 'Revolting Rhymes'; or you could use a nursery rhyme as the basis of a modern story – for example, imagining Little Red Riding Hood or Goldilocks as very contemporary young women, instead of the rather passive victims of the original rhymes. Create something unpredictable and entertaining for an audience of your age or older.

Use:
+ dialogue
+ corny rhymes
+ fast-paced storytelling
+ wacky characters.

ASSESS YOUR LEARNING

- Make a significant contribution to discussion, including evaluating others' ideas
- Use vocabulary precisely and organize your talk to communicate clearly

a) Think about how your participation in the group discussions has improved.

b) What feedback did you receive from the observer(s) in the discussion about the best sitcoms?

c) Identify your strengths and areas for development under these headings, marking your position at the appropriate point in each row.

Individual role

Skill	Area of strength ⟵——————————⟶ Area to develop
Tone	
Volume	
Clarity	
Structure of ideas	
Vocabulary	

Group role

Skill	Area of strength ⟵——————————⟶ Area to develop
Interaction	
Listening	
Pausing	
Got your point across	
Use of eye-contact	
Body language	

- Show understanding of ways in which meaning and information are conveyed in a range of texts

By now you should be feeling increasingly confident at responding to a range of texts. Look at those listed in the grid.

a) Which are you most familiar with?

b) Which would you like more contact with?

Literary texts	Non-fiction
Short stories Novels Poetry	Literary non-fiction: travel writing, autobiography, biography, journals
Drama	Non-fiction: newspaper articles, leaflets, brochures, posters

c) Use your response to identify areas of reading and research in the coming few weeks.

- Write confidently, showing appropriate choices of style in a range of forms
- Use paragraphing and punctuation to make the sequence of ideas clear

If your writing is developing, you should be taking more risks, writing more creatively, expanding your vocabulary, using a wider range of grammatical constructions and writing in more forms than in the past.

Look back at some of your earlier writing (e.g. from the start of the year or last year's lessons) and compare it with some of your recent work.

Using bullet points, summarize:
a) the development you notice
b) the parts of your writing you feel you could develop more.

FINISHING LINE

Britain and other parts of Europe contain many unusual and memorable place names. J.K. Rowling and other writers occasionally borrow them as character names (e.g. Snape and Firenze).

Look at the British place names below. Imagine that they are actually verbs or nouns in a dictionary with specific meanings. Think up some wacky meanings for each word, or think of some other place names to use.

For example:
Kettering (Northants) – (verb) pushing forward in a busy queue

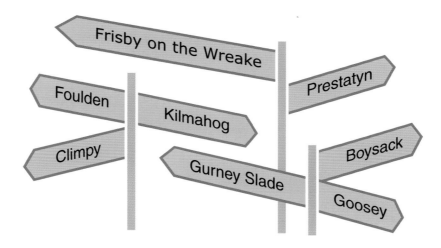

Learning objectives

By the end of this unit you should be able to:

- Show confidence in matching talk to different contexts
- Use standard English confidently when required

- Voice personal and critical responses to poems, showing awareness of different features
- Select and synthesize a range of information from a variety of sources

- Organize ideas into clear paragraphs
- Present your ideas coherently in non-fiction

INTRODUCTION

This unit is about controversial topics, and how difficult it can sometimes be to tell the difference between facts and opinions. The two main topics are corporal punishment and whaling, and they are viewed through a variety of sources, including poems, novels, newpaper reports and opinion pieces.

WARM-UP

1 Wasps are unpopular insects. Read the fact-file below about wasps; then imagine that you work for an advertising agency that has been asked to give wasps a positive image. How would you approach the task?

WASP FACT-FILE

- Wasp is the common name for any of approximately 25,000 insects that have well-defined life stages, separated by a distinct metamorphosis, the adult having a narrow waist between the first and second abdominal segments.

- About 16,000 species of wasps are parasitic, feeding on the bodies or eggs of other insects or of spiders.

- Many different kinds of wasps exist, with widely varying habits and structural characteristics. They may be divided into the social wasps and the solitary wasps. Social wasps include the hornets, the yellow jackets, and the large, mahogany-coloured wasps known as the paper wasps; they live in communities consisting of males, females, and sterile workers.

- The solitary wasps, including the mud daubers, potter wasps, and digger wasps, produce no workers and build individual nests.

- Wasps vary greatly in size. Some of the parasitic wasps are so small that several may develop in a small insect egg. Other species can reach a body length of about 5 cm. The female and worker wasps have a sting, which is used to attack their prey or to protect them against enemies.

- Although adult wasps are largely carnivorous, or meat eaters, some also eat vegetable matter, such as overripe fruit. As a rule, young wasps are fed entirely on other insects or insect remains.

2 This unit includes a debate about whether smacking children should be banned. Attitudes to children always vary. Read through the quotations below and decide
a) which quotation you find the funniest
b) which seems most true or untrue.

I

The thing that impresses me the most about America is the way parents obey their children.

King Edward VIII (1894–1972)

II

A child becomes an adult when he realizes that he has a right not only to be right but also to be wrong.

Thomas Szasz, *The Second Sin* (1973)
'Childhood'

III

Learning to dislike children at an early age saves a lot of expense and aggravation later in life.

Robert Byrne

IV

Somewhere on this globe, every ten seconds, there is a woman giving birth to a child. She must be found and stopped.

Sam Levenson (1911–1980)

V

There was a time when we expected nothing of our children but obedience, as opposed to the present, when we expect everything of them but obedience.

Anatole Broyard

SPARE THE ROD

The three texts in this section are about corporal punishment for children. Text A is a BBC news report about smacking. Text B is an opinion piece in a newspaper in favour of smacking. Text C is an extract from a novel, in which a new teacher loses her temper and beats a young pupil with a cane.

Children in anti-smacking protest

Hundreds of children have marched through central London to demand an end to smacking.

They paraded along the streets of Westminster chanting 'Stop the smacking', and waving placards which read 'Violence is not the answer' and 'We have rights too'.

The children ended their protest at Downing Street, where they handed in a letter addressed to Tony Blair, urging him to ban all physical punishment of children.

The demonstration was organized by children and teenagers from campaign group Article 12, a young people's organisation dedicated to promoting children's rights to expression.

'We want to show the government actively that we are opposed to physical punishment of children,' said one of the organisers, 16-year-old David Henry, from Manchester.

'We want to make a political statement to the whole world that children should not be smacked or hurt in any way by anyone. A lot of the little children who are here today have got a lot to say but they are the ones that don't get listened to.'

Another teenage protester, Kate Wood, from north London, said: 'We believe that all forms of physical punishment are wrong and therefore smacking should be illegal.'

And she criticized government proposals to tighten the law on assaults on children, which stop short of an outright ban.

'The government did a consultation document that was in very complicated language that children could not understand and they did not even bother talking to children about it,' said Kate, 14.

The children were given strong support from a retired chaplain, the Rev Charles Dodd, who said all physical punishment should be banned.

'Smacking is the root of all violence which is current in our society,' he said. 'There is no such thing as a loving smack.'...

In 1998 a survey by the Office of National Statistics found that 88% of parents felt smacking was sometimes necessary but only 7% approved of caning.

Smacking has already been banned in Sweden, Finland, Denmark, Norway, Austria, Cyprus, Croatia and Latvia.

Italy, Germany, Bulgaria, Belgium and the Republic of Ireland are all in the process of legislating against physically rebuking children.

But in the United States the law varies from state to state, with caning still allowed.

From www.news.bbc.co.uk

TEXT B

I was smacked but those short, sharp swipes did me good

by Kitty Dimbleby

The 24-year-old daughter of author Bel Mooney and broadcaster Jonathan Dimbleby recalls an idyllic childhood that was not marred by the occasional smack.

I was smacked as a child. Once. I was six and was behaving terribly at a friend's party – sulking, being rude, refusing to leave and kicking and screaming when asked to. When this continued at home, my frustrated mother grabbed a spoon and struck the back of my hand.

Yes, it hurt, my skin went horribly red and I remember being stunned. But it did the job. I can remember thinking I've pushed Mum too far; yes I felt cross with her, but also with myself, knowing I had behaved abominably.

There was also, it has to be said, the 'flicking'. If Mum lost her temper, she had a powerful weapon in her armoury. She would, like lightening, swat an available body part to break up a sibling argument or general fractiousness.

My older brother, Daniel, and I became experts at dodging it, but when she made contact, it hurt. And she still can't break the habit – my brother remembers a flick at Easter, and he's now 30!

Under proposals passed by the House of Lords this week, parents could face prosecution for all but the gentlest smacks. Bruising, cuts, abrasions, or even making a red mark with the back of a spoon, could all land parents in jail.

But I was never hit as a child – hitting implies a clenched fist, adult violence. A smack is a short, sharp swipe, causing little pain but shocking a child into momentary silence and the long-term realization that the behaviour that provoked the smack was unacceptable.

My memories of my childhood are fairly idyllic. I grew up in Bath and London and although we sometimes had nannies until I was six, I don't remember them. Mum worked from home and was always there to administer love and authority. A far worse punishment than a smack (when I'd thrown food at the babysitter) was not being allowed to climb into bed with my parents to watch telly before going to school.

We have always been a tactile family. Mum would embarrass me with hugs and kisses outside school, and Dad made sure, even though he was always busy working, that he was there to read a bedtime story. But there were rules. Homework straight after school, limited TV, please and thank you always, punctual bedtimes.

There were more serious smackings. As a daddy's girl, the mere idea of a telling-off from my father would be enough, but my brother remembers being properly put across Dad's knee – once. He was about nine, and had had a huge tantrum, then punched Mum and winded her.

Of course, many people find this paradoxical: how can we teach a child not to hit by hitting? But my brother feels it was right. He never hit my mother again and, contrary to reports of the psychological damage smacking can cause, he has never hit anybody and has definitely not turned into a violent young man.

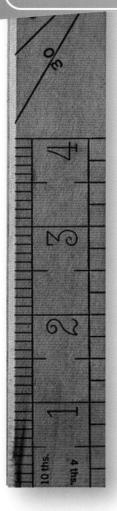

But Mum and Dad never injured us. I believe a lot of my generation – I'm now 24 – wonder what all this fuss is about. Most of my friends' parents used to smack as a last resort and we all agree it was always deserved and, more importantly, it worked.

One friend told me of the time she had a rage in a crowded supermarket and her mother giving her a wallop. She remembers it vividly and likens it to slapping someone who was hysterical.

During our teens, smacking had stopped – by this time 'disappointing' Mum and Dad was enough to prevent bad behaviour. I remember Mum's best friend advising her that the best way to get rid of my awful boyfriend was to stop complaining about him. She was right: as soon as Mum approved, the boy got ditched. But she was fierce about stopping me wearing hot-pants and nail varnish.

Teenage arguments were always explosive but I knew not to push my parents too far. We also talked – about sex, drugs and friends – and I went to my parents for advice about everything and always phoned if I was going to be late.

Mum and Dad were smacked by their parents – we tease my grandmother for spanking Dad with the soft side of a hairbrush, which didn't hurt him in the slightest, and Mum remembers the odd slap on the leg. In their day it was normal: Dad's boarding school and Mum's state primary both allowed use of the ruler, which was worse than anything they could expect at home.

Although Mum and dad grew up at different ends of the class spectrum, their parents had similar attitudes, which they passed on to us. Talking about it now, they say they don't feel guilty, and nor would I expect them to.

Would I smack my children? Probably, but only as a last resort. I honestly don't believe it did me any harm.

 **TEXT C**

In D.H. Lawrence's novel, *The Rainbow*, Ursula Brangwen is a teacher at a small school in Nottinghamshire. It is a job she begins with enthusiasm, but soon comes to loathe, chiefly because of her difficulties in controlling her class. In this extract, Williams – a boy who has persistently irritated and taunted her – pushes her too far …

During the geography lesson, as she was pointing to the map with her cane, the boy continually ducked his whitish head under the desk, and attracted the attention of other boys.

"Williams," she said, gathering her courage, for it was critical now to speak to him, "what are you doing?"

He lifted his face, the sore-rimmed eyes half smiling. There was something intrinsically indecent about him. Ursula shrank away.

"Nothing," he replied, feeling a triumph.

"What are you doing?" she repeated, her heart-beat suffocating her.

"Nothing," replied the boy, insolently, aggrieved, comic.

"If I speak to you again, you must go down to Mr. Harby," she said.

But this boy was a match even for Mr. Harby. He was so persistent, so cringing, and flexible, he howled so when he was hurt, that the master hated more the teacher who sent him than he hated the boy himself. For of the boy he was sick of the sight. Which Williams knew. He grinned visibly.

Ursula turned to the map again, to go on with the geography lesson. But there was a little ferment in the class. Williams' spirit infected them all. She heard a scuffle, and then she trembled inwardly. If they all turned on her this time, she was beaten.

"Please, Miss –" called a voice in distress.

She turned round. One of the boys she liked was ruefully holding out a torn celluloid collar. She heard the complaint, feeling futile.

"Go in front, Wright," she said.

She was trembling in every fibre. A big, sullen boy, not bad but very difficult, slouched out to the front. She went on with the lesson, aware that Williams was making faces at Wright, and that Wright was grinning behind her. She was afraid. She turned to the map again. And she was afraid.

"Please, Miss, Williams—" came a sharp cry, and a boy on the back row was standing up, with drawn, pained brows, half a mocking grin on his pain, half real resentment against Williams— "Please, Miss, he's nipped me," —and he rubbed his leg ruefully.

"Come in front, Williams," she said.

The rat-like boy sat with his pale smile and did not move.

"Come in front," she repeated, definite now.

"I shan't," he cried, snarling, rat-like, grinning. Something went click in Ursula's soul. Her face and eyes set, she went through the class straight. The boy cowered before her glowering, fixed eyes. But she advanced on him, seized him by the arm, and dragged him from his seat. He clung to the form. It was the battle between him and her. Her instinct had suddenly become calm and quick. She jerked him from his grip, and dragged him, struggling and kicking, to the front. He kicked her several times, and clung to the forms as he passed, but she went on. The class was on its feet in excitement. She saw it, and made no move.

She knew if she let go the boy he would dash to the door. Already he had run home once out of her class. So she snatched her cane from the desk, and brought it down on him. He was writhing and kicking. She saw his face beneath her, white, with eyes like the eyes of a fish, stony, yet full of hate and horrible fear. And she loathed him, the hideous writhing thing that was nearly too much for her. In horror lest he should overcome her, and yet at the heart quite calm, she brought down the cane again and again, whilst he struggled making inarticulate noises, and lunging vicious kicks at her. With one hand she managed to hold him, and now and then the cane came down on him. He writhed, like a mad thing. But

the pain of the strokes cut through his writhing, vicious, coward's courage, bit deeper, till at last, with a long whimper that became a yell, he went limp. She let him go, and he rushed at her, his teeth and eyes glinting. There was a second of agonized terror in her heart: he was a beast thing. Then she caught him, and the cane came down on him. A few times, madly, in a frenzy, he lunged and writhed, to kick her. But again the cane broke him, he sank with a howling yell on the floor, and like a beaten beast lay there yelling.

Mr. Harby had rushed up towards the end of this performance.

"What's the matter?" he roared.

Ursula felt as if something were going to break in her.

"I've thrashed him," she said, her breast heaving, forcing out the words on the last breath. The headmaster stood choked with rage, helpless. She looked at the writhing, howling figure on the floor.

"Get up," she said. The thing writhed away from her. She took a step forward. She had realized the presence of the headmaster for one second, and then she was oblivious of it again.

"Get up," she said. And with a little dart the boy was on his feet. His yelling dropped to a mad blubber. He had been in a frenzy.

"Go and stand by the radiator," she said.

As if mechanically, blubbering, he went.

ACTIVITIES

1 Texts A and B both directly address the controversial issue of smacking. Copy and complete the grid below to compare their content and style.

	Text A	Text B
Write down three to five main points that each text makes.		
Select one quotation that sums up the viewpoint of the text.		
Choose one word from the list below that best sums up the written style of the text. Then choose a word that is least appropriate for the text. Words: factual, humorous, lively, informative, opinionated, balanced, subjective, bland, provocative, interesting		
Sketch a picture that captures the main message of the text.		

2 Look again at Text C.
  a) Use a spider diagram to explore and record what we learn about Ursula's character.
  b) Compare your findings with a partner's. Be prepared to justify your conclusions with evidence from the text.

3 Imagine it is some hours after the incident described in Text C. Think about how the different characters may explain what happened. Speak or write a comment from each character, using the sentence starters below. Aim to vary the language according to the speaker.

Sentence starters:
  ✦ Ursula: 'I still can't quite believe what happened …'
  ✦ Williams: 'I'm making a complaint. She just went mad at me …'
  ✦ Mr Harby: 'The first sign that there was a problem was when I heard shouting …'

4 What is your own view of corporal punishment – used by parents and in schools? Write a paragraph expressing your own viewpoint.

WHALE WATCHING

This section is about a practice that many people find barbaric – hunting whales. The texts include some factual pieces, a poem by Heathcote

Williams, and an extract from Herman Melville's novel *Moby Dick*. Read the texts carefully, thinking about the different viewpoints that they express.

The third day… we sighted whales again. We lowered three boats as promptly as usual; but when within about half a mile of the 'pod' some slight noise in one of the boats galled them, and away they went in the wind's eye, it blowing a stiffish breeze at the time. It was from the first evidently a hopeless task to chase them, but we persevered until recalled to the ship, dead beat with fatigue … In passing, I would like to refer to the wonderful way in which these whales realize at a great distance, if the slightest sound be made, the presence of danger. I do not use the word 'hear' because so abnormally small are their organs of hearing, the external opening being quite difficult to find, that I do not believe they *can* hear at all well. But I firmly believe they possess another sense by means of which they are able to detect any unusual vibration of the waves of either air or sea at a far greater distance than it would be possible for them to hear. Whatever this power may be which they possess, all whalemen are well acquainted with their exercise of it, and always take the most elaborate precautions to render their approach to a whale noiseless.

From *The Cruise of the 'Cacholot' Round the World after Sperm Whales* by Frank T. Bullen

The great, intelligent eyes stared back into his; was it pure imagination, or did an almost human sense of fun also lurk in their depths?

Why were these graceful sea-beasts so fond of man, to whom they owed so little. It made one feel that the human race was worth something after all, if it could inspire such unselfish devotion.

From *The Deep Range* by Arthur C. Clarke

TEXT F

Whalenation

by Heathcote Williams

When an underwater shape is detected on the
   submarine radar,
Catcher boats are despatched from the factory-ship.
The harpoon on the raised foredeck is manned
And swivelled in the direction of the whale.

As the whale comes within range,
The engine's screw is slowed down,
And then silenced.

An accurate shot lands between the shoulder-blades.
An inaccurate shot is followed up by two, three or
   four more.

At the end of the five-foot-long steel harpoon
A small serrated cup prevents ricochet.

The tip strikes,
Followed by a time-fused charge exploding three
   seconds later,
Splintering and lacerating the harpoon's way into the
whale's side.

Next to the grenade,
Four barbed flanges pivot on hinges,
And as the whale struggles,
The strain on the rope snaps the barbs open:
They fly out, ripping into the lungs and inner
   organs,
Embedding the harpoon inside the whale,
Anchoring her body.

The whale clashes her jaws together,
Pants, flurries, and spurts blood raspingly through
   her blow-hole.
She thrashes her tail against the surface,
Strenuously heaving at the six-inch-thick nylon line
Attached to accumulator springs in the catcher-
   boat's hold,
Designed to buffer every move.

Twenty minutes pass.
The whale's ribs become too heavy to move.
The whale's rib muscles give up their strength.
The air-valves collapse, admitting a rush of
   sea-water;

The whale's lungs flood.
She suffocates and dies,
Revolving slowly in the water
Leaving her white stomach exposed.

A hollow lance,
Attached to an air-line,
Is fired at her upturned belly,
Feeding compressed air into her corpse,
To inflate it and keep it afloat.

An identifying flag –
With a radar reflector and the catcher-boat's
        number –
Is lobbed into her.

She is left to drift,
Rimmed with oil-slick and blood.

With no enemies in the sea
The whale is loth to believe in the attack,
As were the Indians, as were the aborigines.

The factory-ship, large as an aircraft carrier,
With the capacity to deal with a whale every thirty
        minutes,
Draws alongside.

A hole is bored into the nearest end of her body,
    lips or tail.
A tow-line is attached,
And she is hauled to the bottom of the ramp.

A set of moving claws is lowered towards her.
The hawser wire is pulled.
The curved fingers of the metal tongs bite.

The whale is inched up the slope on to the flensing
    deck.

Wearing spiked plates on their boots to pin
        themselves to the body,
The flensing crew, armed with long-handled knives,
Slice into the whale,
Scoring huge straps, eighteen inches wide and ten
        feet long;

Wires are looped around the ends of the loose flesh,
And winches tear it from the whale's side.

The whale is stuffed through manholes,
To be carved into a sodden mess by whirring knives
That lie below in rotating drums.

The minced flesh is shunted into digester-tanks
And boiled down for four hours by super-heated
        steam.
The solid residue is dried and bagged up.
The oil is piped into the separator house:
Double-boiled, centrifuged,
Hardened into edible fats,
Graded into half a dozen categories,
Barrelled and stored.

On deck, the skull, jaw-bones, ribs, spine and pelvis
Are dismembered with chain-saws,
Then ground down, and shovelled into the
        bone-cookers;
Melted and milled into chicken-feed and fertilisers.

From a whale who was pregnant,
The unborn are dragged into the meat-boilers
With huge hooks slung into their blow-holes.

The inner organs are towed into other boiler
To be distilled into pharmaceuticals.
The skin is collected from the slipways for
        glycerine.
The belly rubber is reserved for a delicacy known as
    'whale bacon'.
The jaw cartilage is pickled.
The tail-flukes are frozen, to be eaten raw.

The floating factory has done little but exchange
        twenty thousand gallons of petroleum
For twenty thousand gallons of animal oil.
Foreign currency has been acquired.
The odd fact that no whale has been found with a
        serious pathological disease,
No whale has ever been found suffering from
        cancerous tumours,
Is overlooked.

TEXT G

It was a sight full of quick wonder and awe! The vast swells of the omnipotent sea; the surging, hollow roar they made, as they rolled along the eight gunwales, like gigantic bowls in a boundless bowling-green; the brief suspended agony of the boat, as it would tip for an instant on the knife-like edge of the sharper waves, that almost seemed threatening to cut it in two; the sudden profound dip into the watery glens and hollows; the keen spurrings and goadings to gain the top of the opposite hill; the headlong, sled-like slide down its other side;– all these, with the cries of the headsmen and harpooneers, and the shuddering gasps of the oarsmen, with the wondrous sight of the ivory Pequod bearing down upon her boats with outstretched sails, like a wild hen after her screaming brood;– all this was thrilling. Not the raw recruit, marching from the bosom of his wife into the fever heat of his first battle; not the dead man's host encountering the first unknown phantom in the other world;– neither of these can feel stranger and stronger emotions than that man does, who for the first time finds himself pulling into the charmed, churned circle of the hunted sperm whale.

The dancing white water made by the chase was now becoming more and more visible, owing to the increasing darkness of the dun cloud-shadows flung upon the sea. The jets of vapor no longer blended, but tilted everywhere to right and left; the whales seemed separating their wakes. The boats were pulled more apart; Starbuck giving chase to three whales running dead to leeward. Our sail was now set, and, with the still rising wind, we rushed along; the boat going with such madness through the water, that the lee oars could scarcely be worked rapidly enough to escape being torn from the row-locks.

Soon we were running through a suffusing wide veil of mist; neither ship nor boat to be seen.

'Give way, men,' whispered Starbuck, drawing still further aft the sheet of his sail; 'there is time to kill a fish yet before the squall comes. There's white water again!– close to! Spring!'

Soon after, two cries in quick succession on each side of us denoted that the other boats had got fast; but hardly were they overheard, when with a lightning-like hurtling whisper Starbuck said: 'Stand up!' and Queequeg, harpoon in hand, sprang to his feet.

Though not one of the oarsmen was then facing the life and death peril so close to them ahead, yet with their eyes on the intense countenance of the mate in the stern of the boat, they knew that the imminent instant had come; they heard, too, an enormous wallowing sound as of fifty elephants stirring in their litter. Meanwhile the boat was still booming through the mist, the waves curling and hissing around us like the erected crests of enraged serpents.

'That's his hump. There, there, give it to him!' whispered Starbuck.

A short rushing sound leaped out of the boat; it was the darted iron of Queequeg. Then all in one welded commotion came an invisible push from astern, while forward the boat seemed striking on a ledge; the sail collapsed and exploded; a gush of scalding vapor shot up near by; something rolled and tumbled like an earthquake beneath us. The whole crew were half suffocated as they were tossed helter-skelter into the white curdling cream of the squall. Squall, whale, and harpoon had all blended together; and the whale, merely grazed by the iron, escaped.

Though completely swamped, the boat was nearly unharmed. Swimming round it we picked up the floating oars, and lashing them across the gunwale, tumbled back to our places. There we sat up to our knees in the sea, the water covering every rib and plank, so that to our downward gazing eyes the suspended craft seemed a coral boat grown up to us from the bottom of the ocean.

The wind increased to a howl; the waves dashed their bucklers together; the whole squall roared, forked, and crackled around us like a white fire upon the prairie, in which, unconsumed, we were burning; immortal in these jaws of death! In vain we hailed the other boats; as well roar to the live coals down the chimney of a flaming furnace as hail those boats in that storm. Meanwhile the driving scud, rack, and mist, grew darker with the shadows of night; no sign of the ship could be seen. The rising sea forbade all attempts to bale out the boat. The oars were useless as propellers, performing now the office of life-preservers. So, cutting the lashing of the waterproof match keg, after many failures Starbuck contrived to ignite the lamp in the lantern; then stretching it on a waif pole, handed it to Queequeg as the standard-bearer of this forlorn hope. There, then, he sat, holding up that imbecile candle in the heart of that almighty forlornness. There, then, he sat, the sign and symbol of a man without faith, hopelessly holding up hope in the midst of despair.

Wet, drenched through, and shivering cold, despairing of ship or boat, we lifted up our eyes as the dawn came on. The mist still spread over the sea, the empty lantern lay crushed in the bottom of the boat. Suddenly Queequeg started to his feet, hollowing his hand to his ear. We all heard a faint creaking, as of ropes and yards hitherto muffled by the storm. The sound came nearer and nearer; the thick mists were dimly parted by a huge, vague form. Affrighted, we all sprang into the sea as the ship at last loomed into view, bearing right down upon us within a distance of not much more than its length.

Floating on the waves we saw the abandoned boat, as for one instant it tossed and gaped beneath the ship's bows like a chip at the base of a cataract; and then the vast hull rolled over it, and it was seen no more till it came up weltering astern. Again we swam for it, were dashed against it by the seas, and were at last taken up and safely landed on board. Ere the squall came close to, the other boats had cut loose from their fish and returned to the ship in good time. The ship had given us up, but was still cruising, if haply it might light upon some token of our perishing,– an oar or a lance pole.

From *Moby Dick* by Herman Melville

The men had to work over the side, walking about in spike boots on the whale carcasses themselves … It was an incredibly wasteful business in those days. Only the blubber was used and the 'skrotts', as the stripped carcasses were called, were cast adrift in the harbour. They floated ashore to rot on the beaches and to this day Deception Harbour, and many of the bays and inlets of South Georgia, are edged with ramparts of bleached bones, skulls, jaws, backbones and ribs, memorials to that uncontrolled slaughter. They bear witness to the greed and folly of mankind. At the shore whaling stations, too, similar profligate waste at first prevailed until the Government intervened to stop it.

From *Lost Leviathan*
by F.D Ommanney

ACTIVITIES

1 Think about what we learn about whales from this collection of texts. Copy and complete the grid below to catalogue your response to the texts. Put a tick or cross in the appropriate column.

	D	E	F	G	H
Does the text describe the whale's appearance?					
Does the text show the grandeur and majesty of whales?					
Does the text show humans admiring whales?					
Does the text show the power of whales?					
Does the text show the brutality of humans?					
Does the text leave us admiring whales?					
Does the text leave us admiring humans?					

2 Look at Text G. It is the oldest text in the collection. Find four clues from the text that tell you it was written long ago: look for specific words or sentences.

3 Think about the facts that you learn from the texts. Sketch out the content of a fact sheet that draws together key information about:
a) whales
b) the process of whaling.
✦ Focus on the content, rather than the detail of the visuals and text.
✦ Think carefully about how to organize your material in a way that will interest and inform your reader.

4 People have strong views about whaling. Draw up a list of arguments for and against whaling. Use material from the texts, as well as your own ideas.

5 Look more closely at Heathcote Williams's poem about whaling, which is a powerful piece of descriptive writing.

  a) With a partner, discuss what makes a poem, a poem. Consider:
   + rhyme
   + rhythm
   + emotive vocabulary
   + frequent use of adjectives and adverbs
   + strong imagery
   + appropriate subject matter (e.g. nature)
   + short lines (i.e. to look like a poem, not prose).

  b) Talk about whether Heathcote Williams's text can be described as a poem, rather than a prose description set out like a poem.

> **Glossary**
>
> **Prose** – the writing we find in novels, drama and non-fiction. Writing that is not poetry.

UNIT CHALLENGES

1. Talk show

Imagine a daytime television discussion programme, with guests and a studio audience. After the guests have been interviewed about whether they think that smacking children is acceptable, members of the audience are asked for their opinions.

The following characters are in the audience:

Pensioner, Ernie Raven	Thinks it's time children were taught how to behave properly. Strongly supports smacking
Parent, Philippa Nettleton	Believes it should be left to parents to decide
Psychologist, Carlos Tate	Believes physical punishment as a child can have a damaging long-term effect on self-esteem
Politician, Sarah Rees	Believes that in a modern society, physical punishment has no place
Politician, Stephen Parkinson	Believes it's not up to the Government to decide people's rights

a) Make notes on how each character would respond to the question: 'Do you think smacking is acceptable?' Consider their language, tone, vocabulary, level of formality, etc.

b) In pairs, take turns to play the role of interviewer and the characters. This will help you to practise speaking in a range of styles.

c) Ask your partner (or another listener) how effectively you changed the language according to each speaker.

2. Making a speech

Imagine a parliamentary debate in which MPs are going to vote on whether smacking should be banned. As a member of parliament, you have been called upon to make a three-minute speech that wins over your audience.

a) Choose whether to argue for or against a ban on smacking.

b) Research the topic. Don't make it just assertions (opinions); include facts and statistics (such as other countries which have or haven't taken the same measures).

c) Plan a structure: what are your main points? How will you organize and link them?

d) Draft your speech. Remember that it will be delivered aloud, not read, so keep sentences to a reasonable length. Use some short sentences for impact. Use connecting phrases to help your listeners to follow your argument (e.g. 'The second reason for outlawing smacking is …'

3. Controversy

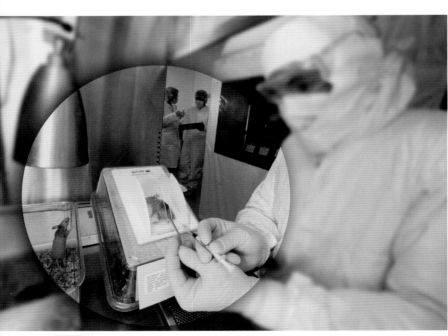

a) Choose a topic that people feel strongly about, an issue with strong arguments on both sides. Here are some possibilities:
  + Why eating meat is wrong
  + Why school uniform represses pupils' individualism
  + Why smoking in public places should be outlawed
  + Why all experiments on animals should be banned

b) Put together a briefing sheet that is designed to:
  + teach the main facts about the issue
  + present both sides of the issue.

Think about the best way to present the material. Consider the use of:

+ headings and subheadings
+ images
+ questions and answers
+ quotations and statistics
+ bullet points
+ different fonts
+ boxes.

Aim to produce a balanced text, even though you may have strong personal feelings about the issue. It will be assessed on how well you organize your material and how objective it is.

4. Writing a dual narrative

In the extract from *The Rainbow*, we see Ursula Brangwen losing her temper with an unruly student. We see the event mainly from Ursula's viewpoint. However, some novelists use dual narratives to convey more than one viewpoint – so we swap from one narrator to another, often retelling the same incident.

Write the opening sequence of a short story or novel set in a school. Imagine a new teacher facing an unknown class for the first time. Use a dual narrative to tell the story.

Your two opening paragraphs could start like this:

Paragraph 1:   As I pushed open the classroom door, I knew there could be no turning back ...

Paragraph 2:   The classroom door opened, slowly, a bit hesitantly; we fell quiet in expectation ...

The challenge is to create a powerful scene, full of tension and psychological interest rather than action.

+ Hint at what might happen later, but – for now – keep the reader guessing.
+ Describe details of the room, the teacher and the students. Help the reader to imagine what the atmosphere is like.
+ Aim for controlled, precise use of language.

ASSESS YOUR LEARNING

- Show confidence in matching talk to different contexts
- Use standard English confidently when required

Record how your spoken work is developing and in which contexts you are making most progress by rating each area, listed below, from A to C.
A = strong, C = weak.

Grouping	Context
Solo	Impromptu discussion
Paired	Prepared talk
Small group	Structured debate
Large group	Being in role as a character
Class or bigger	Interviewing
	Chairing a meeting
	Being interviewed
	Problem-solving
	Giving feedback
	Listening to others

- Voice personal and critical responses to poems, showing awareness of different features
- Select and synthesize a range of information from a variety of sources

a) Think about how you responded to Heathcote Williams's poem about whaling. How did its poetic features make you respond to the message of the poem?

b) This unit has given you practice in reading and synthesizing (combining) information. Decide which parts of the process you are best at and which you need more practice with:
   - reading
   - finding information
   - identifying parts of a text that are relevant/important
   - knowing how to present information.

- Organize ideas into clear paragraphs
- Present your ideas coherently in non-fiction

a) Look at the non-fiction texts you have written over the past few weeks or months. How could you improve on the presentation of these non-fiction texts? Consider:

- layout features (e.g. use of bullet points, boxes, shading)
- use of language (sentence length, type of vocabulary, type of connectives)
- organization (use of paragraphs, chronological or non-chronological presentation of material).

b) Tick the text types, listed below, which you have covered successfully.

- leaflet
- newspaper article
- poster
- fact sheet
- persuasive pamphlet
- travel writing
- autobiography
- recipe

c) Which text types do you need more practice in?

FINISHING LINE

Look at the three images below. Each one is a picture of a well-known phrase in English. Work out what they are. Then sketch out three more cartoons to represent other familiar phrases and ask your friends to guess them.

some**I'M**thing

JOanB

Somewhere

RAINBOW

Learning objectives

By the end of this unit you should be able to:

- Make significant contributions in discussions, evaluating others' ideas and varying how and when you participate
- Use vocabulary precisely and confidently to communicate clearly

- Show understanding of ways in which meaning and information are conveyed
- Identify and analyse argument, opinion and alternative interpretations

- Use grammatical features and vocabulary accurately and effectively
- Write non-fiction that is coherent and gives clear points of view

INTRODUCTION

This unit looks at the way we try to persuade people to do or believe things. It explores different forms of advertising, polemical writing (writing with a strong persuasive message) and speeches.

(WARM-UP)

1   Read the quotation below; then discuss the questions with a partner.

> 'The real challenge for advertisers is that people have all the products they need. All the essentials have been invented, such as cars, computers, soap and shampoo. All we can do is to persuade people that they need better, faster, newer or cleaner versions. We need to persuade them that they need something that they don't yet realize they want.'
>
> *Ian Miles*, Advertising Consultant

a) Think of some products we take for granted nowadays, but which people didn't have 20 years ago.
b) What do you think is the most unnecessary product that you have ever seen for sale?
c) When have you bought a new version of an item because you wanted a 'better, faster, newer or cleaner' model?

2   Read the quotations about advertising on the opposite page. Then discuss:
   ✦ what you understand by each one
   ✦ which you agree/disagree with
   ✦ which is funniest or most true.

I

Advertising may be described as the science of arresting the human intelligence long enough to get money from it.
Anonymous

II

Advertising is the modern substitute for argument; its function is to make the worse appear the better.
George Santayana

III

Many a small thing has been made large by the right kind of advertising.
Mark Twain

IV

What is the difference between unethical and ethical advertising? Unethical advertising uses falsehoods to deceive the public; ethical advertising uses truth to deceive the public.
Vilhjalmur Stefanss

SELLING A LIFESTYLE

There are many ways in which advertisers persuade us to buy a product or believe a new idea. They often do this by portaying an appealing lifestyle which the consumer can 'buy into'. The texts here include a cycle advert from the mid-1900s, a magazine advert for an exercise machine, and a non-fiction account of the ingredients in fast food.

CYCLING

Many people look on cycling as hard work and something to be avoided, but remember, it is only as hard as you make it for yourself. Given the right approach it is the finest of all outdoor pastimes, healthy exercise, fresh air ad lib and the most economical of all transport. As an enthusiast for nearly forty years I should know and I can help you to enjoy many happy hours awheel by advising you on acquiring a suitable riding position which is one of the most important things, the proper equipment for your type of cycling and also the most suitable machine. We are agents for Phillips Cycles and there is one in their range to suit the majority. For the enthusiast who already knows what he or she wants we build the finest lightweight frames available in Reynolds "531" tubing and many lug designs. These frames can be made to your own specification regarding angles, wheelbase, etc, etc. We also carry a large stock of touring bags, tyres and most other things for the bicycle. Our repair service is second to none, prompt, reasonable in cost and all work done by an expert. Frames re-enamelled, chromium plating, wheel building, in fact the lot.

Note the address for the best service in London: —

H. R. MORRIS
Cycle Maker

All Accessories   C. T. C., N.C.U. Approved Repairer
28 ORFORD ROAD, WALTHAMSTOW, E.17
Telephone: COPpermill 2282

TEXT B

The Weapon of Mass Reduction

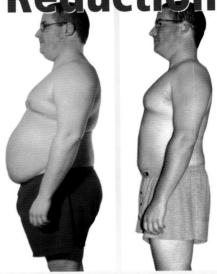

David after just 3 months regular training on the Indoor Rower

"Earlier this year, I appeared on Channel 4's Fit Farm, which was broadcast every week day for 12 weeks, ending in May 2004. Upon entering I was 16 stone 1 pound, which at 5 foot 5" is not impressive!

"After our initial gym equipment training I knew that the Concept 2 Indoor Rower was the tool for me to achieve my goals. It works every major muscle group, so is great for all round fitness. It is an amazing feeling and you can really feel the difference in the muscles, especially the legs, triceps, shoulders and abs (in fact as a direct result of the rowing machine I have the start of a six-pack!).

"The Indoor Rower is also fantastic for rehabilitation as there is no impact, which was a major plus for me as I have bad knees due to skiing injuries.

"I would put 70% of my success down to rowing. The results it gave me were amazing. I lost more weight as a percentage of my body weight than any other guest in the Fit Farm. I was also the only one to use the Concept 2 as my main piece of equipment, which is probably no coincidence. In all, I lost 22% of my body weight in total, taking me to 12 stone 7 pounds.

"After coming out of the Fit Farm I was committed to carrying on with my fitness and rowing. As well as training by myself I have started up a Sunday morning exercise club with some friends and they all come to my house to have a 2,000 metre rowing competition on my Indoor Rower, which they all love. My aim now is to lose another 5 kilograms so that I can compete as a lightweight in the AXA PPP healthcare British Indoor Rowing Championship later this year.

"I strongly believe that if you only ever buy one piece of cardio equipment it should be the Indoor Rower as it is the most effective form of exercise I know. Quite simply, it's changed my life."

– David Pearce

The Concept 2 Indoor Rower is the world's best selling rowing machine and was recently voted the Best Home Fitness Product by UltraFit magazine readers.

Not only does it provided the ultimate workout, it's built to match. With over 20 years experience of making rowing machines, we're the acknowledged leaders in the field.

And now, with the introduction of the 'Model D' it is even better. It is quieter and smoother to use, offers a broader range of resistance, and features an ergonomically designed handle. It also has an amazingly smart and user-friendly Performance Monitor that sets a new standard in performance feedback.

So, it's Smarter, Friendlier and Quieter and still the same fantastic value for money.

Rental & payment Options Available
www.concept2.co.uk

Concept 2 indoor rower model D
Concept 2 Ltd., Vermont House, Nott'm Sth. & Wilford Ind. Est., Ruddington Lane, Nottingham NG11 7HQ
Tel: 0115 945 5522 Fax: 0115 945 5533 email: info@concept2.co.uk
web: www.concept2.co.uk

From the *Independent* Magazine

TEXT C

The taste of McDonald's french fries has long been praised by customers, competitors, and even food critics. James Beard loved McDonald's fries. Their distinctive taste does not stem from the type of potatoes that McDonald's buys, the technology that processes them, or the restaurant equipment that fries them. Other chains buy their french fries from the same large processing companies, use Russet Burbanks, and have similar fryers in their restaurant kitchens. The taste of a fast food fry is largely determined by the cooking oil. For decades, McDonald's cooked its french fries in a mixture of about 7 percent cottonseed oil and 98 percent beef tallow. The mix gave the fries their unique flavour – and more saturated beef fat per ounce than a McDonald's hamburger.

Amid a barrage of criticism over the amount of cholesterol in their fries, McDonald's switched to pure vegetable oil in 1990. The switch presented the company with an enormous challenge: how to make fries that subtly taste like beef without cooking them in tallow. A look at the ingredients now used in preparation of McDonald's french fries suggests how the problem was solved. Toward the end of the list is a seemingly innocuous, yet oddly mysterious phrase: "natural flavor". That ingredient helps to explain not only why the fries taste so good, but also why most fast food – indeed, most of the food Americans eat today – tastes the way it does.

Open your refrigerator, your freezer, your kitchen cupboards, and look at the labels on your food. You'll find "natural flavor" or "artificial flavor" in just about every list of ingredients. The similarities between these two broad categories of flavor are far more significant than their differences. Both are man-made additives that give most processed food most of its taste. The initial purchase of a food item may be driven by its packaging or appearance, but subsequent purchases are determined mainly by its taste. About 90 percent of the money that Americans spend on food is used to buy processed food. But the canning, freezing, and dehydrating techniques used to process food destroy most of its flavor. Since the end of World War II, a vast industry has arisen in the United States to make processed food palatable. Without this flavor industry, today's fast food industry could not exist. The names of the leading American fast food chains and the bestselling menu items have become famous worldwide, embedded in our popular culture. Few people, however, can name the companies that manufacture fast food's taste.

From *Fast Food Nation*
by Eric Schlosser

ACTIVITIES

I Look at Texts A and B. Text A appeared in a school brochure in 1958. Text B appeared in the *Independent* Magazine.

a) What do you think is the unique selling point of each product (the one thing it can offer that other items cannot)?

b) Who do you think is the target audience?

c) What persuasive techniques are used? Think about design, the way it addresses the reader, formality of language, and the use of quotations.

2 Look more closely at Text A.

a) How can you tell that the advert is not modern? Pick out at least three features of design and use of language as examples.

b) Imagine H.R. Morris has been fast-forwarded into the present. Give him advice on how to update his advert for a modern audience. Show him:
  ✦ how his advert should look
  ✦ how the language should be updated (e.g. think of a slogan; use emotive adjectives such as exciting, fashionable, fast, amazing)
  ✦ how he needs fewer words and a less personal tone.

Present your ideas in one of the following forms:
  ✦ a poster
  ✦ a set of notes
  ✦ a PowerPoint presentation
  ✦ a role play (one person taking the role of the advertiser; another taking the role of a slightly confused H.R. Morris).

3 Look at the design of Text B. What effect do the listed features have on the advert?
  ✦ heading
  ✦ text
  ✦ before and after photographs
  ✦ information box

4 Which of the following would you say is the main message of Text B?
  ✦ The equipment is attractive.
  ✦ The equipment is modern.
  ✦ The equipment is healthy.
  ✦ The equipment is necessary.

5 Look again at Text C.

a) What did you learn from this text about the making of fast food?

b) How would you describe the tone of the author's writing: aggressive, funny, angry, sarcastic, entertaining, factual, dismissive? Write a sentence to explain your choice of description.

6 Choose one of the Texts A to C for analysis. Draw up a three-column grid. In the first column, note what you like about the text; in the second column, note what you don't like; and in the third column, suggest how the message of the text could be made more effective.

What you like	What you don't like	How to improve the text

SPEECH MAKERS

Speeches are important in many aspects of life, such as politics, law and education. Speeches in the House of Commons and Lords contribute to making new laws; barristers and solicitors use speeches in courtrooms; some teaching takes place through speeches (e.g. lectures at college and university).

This section presents the work of two great speakers: Sir Winston Churchill (British Prime Minister for most of the Second World War) and Ronald Reagan (President of the USA during the 1980s). But before you read the speeches of these men, read the advice given in Text D. It is from an old book called *The Manual of Public Speaking*. Then compare the two speeches by Sir Winston Churchill and Ronald Reagan in Texts E and F.

Planning a speech

There are three ways to plan a speech. The first and best method is to go mentally over the subject on which you have to talk and merely think of what you intend to say. And, then, when the time comes, to say it.

Though this is the plan adopted by most of the best speakers, it is not one that the novice should attempt, for the very simple reason that, when the time comes, he won't say it. All the clever ideas that he planned, all the carefully built up arguments that he had prepared, all the amusing side-lights that he had in mind – all of them fly from his brain, as he stands up and gazes on the sea of faces, and everything becomes a total blank. We have experienced it all, so we know.

The second way of planning a speech is to think out all the things that have to be said and to jot down a list of headings on a slip of paper. The slip can then be used while the speech is actually delivered. The headings will keep you on the right lines, they will help you to remember all your points, and they will not cramp your style. In other words, they will assist and not restrict you. This is usually considered as good a way as any of preparing a speech.

The third method is to sit down and write out what you intend to say from beginning to end. You can, then, take your script into a private room and go over it aloud a dozen, or, perhaps, forty times, until you have learnt much of it by heart, while the rest you can fill in by a system of paraphrasing. A glance at the paper, just before you rise to speak, will refresh your memory splendidly and, quite likely, you will be surprised and pleased at your powers of oratory, after the event.

But, if you do go to the trouble of writing out the whole of the speech, do not be tempted to read it on the great occasion. No speech that is read is as convincing as one that is delivered, while many are simply grotesque.

From *The Manual of Public Speaking* by Patrick Pringle

TEXT E

Churchill's war speeches, with their fighting spirit and their denial of the possibility of defeat, rallied the British at the most important period of the war, when Hitler was advancing to Dunkirk and threatening to invade England.

WE HAVE BEFORE US AN ORDEAL OF THE most grievous kind. We have before us many, many long months of struggle and of suffering. You ask, what is our policy? I will say: It is to wage war, by sea, land and air, with all our might and with all the strength that God can give us: to wage war against a monstrous tyranny, never surpassed in the dark, lamentable catalogue of human crime. That is our policy. You ask, What is our aim? I can answer in one word: Victory – victory at all costs, victory in spite of all terror, victory, however long and hard the road may be; for without victory, there is no survival. Let that be realized; no survival for the British Empire; no survival for all that the British Empire has stood for, no survival for the urge and impulse of the ages, that mankind will move forward towards its goal. But I take up my task with buoyancy and hope. I feel sure that our cause will not be suffered to fail among men. At this time I feel entitled to claim the aid of all, and I say, 'Come, then, let us go forward together with our united strength.'

Winston Churchill, speech in the House of Commons, 13 May 1940

TEXT F

This speech was delivered by President Ronald Reagan forty years after the invasion of Normandy beaches by the Allies.

We're here to mark that day in history when the Allied peoples joined in battle to reclaim this continent to liberty. For four long years, much of Europe had been under a terrible shadow. Free nations had fallen, Jews cried out in the camps, millions cried out for liberation. Europe was enslaved, and the world prayed for its rescue. Here in Normandy the rescue began. Here the Allies stood and fought against tyranny in a giant undertaking unparalleled in human history.

We stand on a lonely, windswept point on the northern shore of France. The air is soft, but forty years ago at this moment, the air was dense with smoke and the cries of men, and the air was filled with the crack of rifle fire and the

roar of cannon. At dawn, on the morning of the 6th of June 1944, 225 Rangers jumped off the British landing craft and ran to the bottom of these cliffs. Their mission was one of the most difficult and daring of the invasion: to climb these sheer and desolate cliffs and take out the enemy guns. The Allies had been told that some of the mightiest of these guns were here and they would be trained on the beaches to stop the Allied advance.

The Rangers looked up and saw the enemy soldiers – at the edge of the cliffs shooting down at them with machine-guns and throwing grenades. And the American Rangers began to climb. They shot rope ladders over the face of these cliffs and began to pull themselves up. When one Ranger fell, another would take his place. When one rope was cut, a Ranger would grab another and begin his climb again. They climbed, shot back, and held their footing. Soon, one by one, the Rangers pulled themselves over the top, and in seizing the firm land at the top of these cliffs, they began to seize back the continent of Europe. Two hundred and twenty-five came here. After two days of fighting only ninety could still bear arms.

Behind me is a memorial that symbolizes the Ranger daggers that were thrust into the top of these cliffs. And before me are the men who put them there.

These are the boys of Pointe du Hoc. These are the men who took the cliffs. These are the champions who helped free a continent. These are the heroes who helped end a war.

Gentlemen, I look at you and I think of the words of Stephen Spender's poem. You are men who in your 'lives fought for the life ... and left the vivid air signed with your honor'...

Forty summers have passed since the battle that you fought here. You were young the day you took these cliffs; some of you were hardly more than boys, with the deepest joys of life before you. Yet you risked everything here. Why? Why did you do it? What impelled you to put aside the instinct for self-preservation and risk your lives to take these cliffs? What inspires all the men of the armies that met here? We look at you, and somehow we know the answer. It was faith, and belief; it was loyalty and love.

The men of Normandy had faith that what they were doing was right, faith that they fought for all humanity, faith that a just God would grant them mercy on this beachhead or on the next. It was the deep knowledge – and pray God we have not lost it – that there is a profound moral difference between the use of force for liberation and the use of force for conquest. You were here to liberate, not to conquer, and so you and those others did not doubt your cause. And you were right not to doubt.

You all knew that some things are worth dying for. One's country is worth dying for, and democracy is worth dying for, because it's the most deeply honourable form of government ever devised by man. All of you loved liberty. All of you were willing to fight tyranny, and you knew the people of your countries were behind you.

ACTIVITIES

1 Refer to Text D.
   a) What would you say were the three main pieces of advice given by Patrick Pringle?
   b) What do you agree with?
   c) What do you disagree with?

2 If you were writing a paragraph of advice on making a speech – for example, to a friend who is about to lead an assembly – what tone would you use? Would it be formal or informal? Write the opening few sentences.

3 Look at Texts E and F. Use the grid below to compare the techniques used in the speeches.

	Text E	Text F
How does the speaker involve the audience?		
How does he use varied types and lengths of sentences to create interesting rhythms?		
How does he use vocabulary to help us to visualize what he says (e.g. metaphors and similes)?		
How does he create a sense of emotion?		
Which is your favourite line or image?		

4 Which speech do you admire more? Explain your choice carefully.

5 These historical speeches were written more than 40 years apart. How can you tell that they were written in the past?

POLEMICAL WRITING

Polemical writing expresses a strong attack or defence of a particular viewpoint. Unlike a discursive essay, which weighs up both sides of the argument, polemical writing conveys a single, personal view, often on a controversial subject.

Texts G and H were written for the *Times Educational Supplement*, a weekly newspaper aimed at people who work in schools. Over several weeks it ran a series of debates on controversial issues. Texts G and H are the arguments for and against compulsory school uniform (following a pronouncement by the Education Secretary at that time, Charles Clarke, that all schools should insist on uniform). Text I was a letter written in response to the articles.

TEXT G

Is Clarke right on uniform?

The Education Secretary has launched a war on scruffiness. But is it really such a smart move?

Yes

Geoff Barton

Mention uniform and – like a second-rate school debate – you hear the knee-jerk response about it being an upper-class thing.

The *Daily Telegraph*, for example, hailed Charles Clarke's recent exhortation for schools to have uniforms as "a return to traditional school uniforms, the house system and competitive sport". It was, the paper said, intended to "make comprehensives more like sought-after fee-paying schools".

Predictably the *Telegraph* associates uniform with private schools and poshness. For me – a strong supporter of school uniform- that's a side issue.

Here are five better arguments.

1. Pride and identity

The most successful organisations have a strong self-identity. Their customers and employees know who they are and what they stand for. Uniform reinforces a sense of belonging to the corporate whole. It associates students with our high expectations, whatever their circumstances. It therefore shows our commitment to achieving the best for each child irrespective of background.

2. Individuality

Don't be fooled by arguments that uniform suppresses personality. I watched a group of boys at a school concert the other night. They all wore the same Adidas caps and sports outfits. They weren't expressing personal identity: they were showing which tribe they belonged to. It was their out-of-school uniform.

By dispensing with uniform we pander to media which encourage young people to judge people by how they look, not who they actually are. Watch a few commercials between teen-oriented programmes. Notice the consistent and insidious message that you are a social reject if you aren't wearing the right sunglasses, drinking the right cola, or sporting the fashionable brand. As educators we need to rise above this label culture. Let's enable our young people to define themselves by who they are, not superficially, by the brand names they buy.

3. Community spirit

Uniform encourages a healthy sense of citizenship. Conformism is not fashionable: we live in an age that encourages us to think that all rebellion and defiance is a sign of strong personality. But schools rely on co-operation. We need clear rules to work effectively. Our young people need to learn that conforming isn't some heretical act of weakness, but part of a commitment to being in a community. Wearing a uniform reinforces this.

4. Self-esteem

Uniform breeds self-esteem – and not just for the students. A recent Department of Education and Skills survey shows that 83 per cent of parents favour uniform. It reassures them that the school has high standards and clear expectations of behaviour. Critics might wish to dispute this – though they'll find it hard to find a high-performing English state school that doesn't insist on uniform – but they need to remember the importance of perception.

Falling crime figures and fewer train delays aren't much good if not accompanied by the perception that crime is falling and more trains are on time. That's why so many new heads at failing schools use uniform to change community perceptions of the school and rebuild students' self-esteem.

5. Behaviour

In that famous New York "broken windows" policing policy, officers paid attention to minor vandalism and graffiti and found more serious crimes dropped.

Similarly, when I pick up a student at school for breaching the uniform code by wearing jewellery or trainers, I'm focusing on a small, uncontroversial detail. Looking after these minor issues will often prevent a slide into more serious bad behaviour. It reinforces a culture of personal responsibility.

Uniform isn't a superficial issue separate from learning. As school leaders are increasingly accepting in Australia and the United States, it's a way to state our values and expectations. In saying that students have to be dressed appropriately for lessons, we draw a line between our expectations and the culture of the streets or housing estates around us. This is nothing to do with poshness. It's about focusing on young people as individuals – valuing them for who they are, not how they look.

Pupils need to learn that conforming isn't some heretical act of weakness.

Geoff Barton is headteacher at King Edward VI School, Bury St Edmunds

---

No
Kate Petty

So 66 per cent of respondents to a Department for Education and Skills survey thought uniforms could improve school standards, did they?

That would be nice and simple to fix, wouldn't it? I'm all for easy-to-wash, easy-to-throw-on-in-the-morning clothes for school, but when exactly did the powers-that-be lose faith in the ability of the average parent and child to choose their own clothes – as they do in most of Europe and the United States?

It seems to me that everything a uniform is supposed to fix should be fixed by some other, more fundamental means. Take class difference: is our class system still so rigid that it needs ironing out by dressing children alike? It doesn't work, anyway – we all know the subtle differences children can make to uniforms to show where they belong in the pecking order.

But when all children have been subjected to our current obsession with branding (coupled with the other obsession with league tables) those uniforms are only going to exacerbate the class differences between schools. Everyone will know that the kids in red go to a better school than the kids in blue; that the school with the elaborate uniform and the straw boater is more expensive than the one with the purple blazer. (That was one of the reasons for uniform in the first place, wasn't it?)

I asked my daughter (comprehensive school, no uniform) if she would have preferred a uniform.

She could only say, not entirely seriously of course, that if her school had a uniform, gang warfare with neighbouring schools would soon break out. My son (grammar school, uniform) was not the only one to remove blazer and tie on the bus home for the same reason.

Do we want to give children any more reasons to discriminate against one another? Is that the "sense of identity" we want to encourage? The same one that manifests itself in white and red flag-flying?

Footballers wear a uniform, of course, so you can see which side they play for. So do police officers, so you know who is in authority, and nurses, so you know who is trained to wield a syringe. But schoolchildren? We know who they are, don't we? They are the children around the place, the ones who need protecting and guiding by society as a whole.

Can pride in a school, a positive ethos, discipline, really come from a uniform? Surely it's the other way around?

A good school creates its ethos by taking pleasure in the individuality of its pupils. Doesn't good discipline arise from respecting those differences? Don't children take pride in their school because it is a good institution to belong to?

As a children's author I often talk to schoolchildren, sometimes to one group after another all day long in a hot library. And do you know which groups make my heart sink? The elaborately uniformed ones, who are so often listless and devoid of curiosity, and so often accompanied by bored teachers.

Which groups ask the best questions? The lumbering, straggling, varied and often scruffy children in their own clothes, whose individuality shines off them, reminding me as a speaker that I am in the company of a huge range of thinkers and opinions. (Apologies to all those great kids I've spoken to who were wearing uniforms. You know who you are.)

That's my one-off personal response, I know, but aren't all teachers affected in a similar way every day?

Most grown-ups can recall the horrors of having to spend their teenage years in a hideous and unflattering uniform, not to mention the petty rules surrounding it. Many of my generation can also remember the struggle to avoid the indignity of wearing my brother's girlfriend's cast-offs. Eighty-three per cent of parents might approve of uniform – it's certainly cheaper these days – but I'm not sure we should kid ourselves it's actually for the children's benefit.

I think we should take the heat out of clothes and fashion by letting children wear what they choose to school. They'll very quickly create their own uniforms anyway, but at least that will be their choice and their expression of their own identities.

Don't swallow myths about power of uniform

I am the head of a large comprehensive that shares the same name as Geoff Barton's school ("Is Clarke right on uniform?", TES, July 23). Sadly we have nothing else in common.

In September 2003 we became a no-uniform school and one year later and with no surprise it has been a success. The rhetoric that Mr Barton uses smacks of the *Daily Mail*.

The decision to abandon uniform was a brave step by the governors and there was considerable resistance from the parents and the local community. The usual emotive and unfounded evidence was thrown at us in a similar way to the points raised by Mr Barton. People selectively quote statistics, ignoring the ones that question uniform and completely ignoring the views of the students.

We consulted widely with the student body who were more thoughtful and reflective than a number of their parents.

To all those schools that are considering getting rid of uniform let me reassure you that it has not created fashion wars and behaviour has not deteriorated.

Students are proud of their school. There has not been one incident of dress-related bullying and the regular confrontations between teachers and students about uniform are a thing of the past.

A significant distraction to our core task of learning and teaching has been removed. We are more confident with students who are happier without the uniform, and the whole place is a more attractive and normal environment.

Don't be fooled by the likes of Messrs Barton and Charles Clarke. The civilised world does not stop when you abandon school uniform.

Stephen Jones
Principal of King Edward VI Community College, Totnes, Devon

1 Make a note of the main arguments for or against school uniform that the writers of Texts G and H use.

2 Kate Petty and Geoff Barton use very different styles of writing to approach the topic.
a) How do their writing styles differ?
b) Which do you find more effective?

3 Which of the following words would you use to describe the tone in Text I: angry, indignant, assertive, aggressive, upset, clear, calm, passionate?

4 Look more closely at the language used by ONE of the writers of Texts G to I. Using a spider diagram, make notes on:
   ✦ structure of the argument
   ✦ choice of vocabulary
   ✦ sentence types
   ✦ tone

+ use of effects such as humour, metaphor, simile, hyperbole (deliberate exaggeration)
+ reference to own experience.

UNIT CHALLENGES

1. Debate

Choose one of the topics below and organize a debate in which, working with a partner, you act as the proposition (arguing in favour) or opposition (arguing against).

Topic 1

Imagine that your school wants to promote healthy eating and drinking. It also earns more than £10,000 a year from selling crisps, chocolate and sugary carbonated drinks from vending machines. Without this income, there would be worse facilities for students. But by keeping the machines, the school is undermining its policy on healthy eating.

Motion: 'This house would ban vending machines containing unhealthy food and drink from schools.'

Topic 2

Advertisers currently promote fast food, sweets and other 'unhealthy' products during TV viewing targeted at young children. They have been criticized by health groups. Some people say it is up to parents to control the diets of their children, not advertisers.

Motion: 'This House would ban all advertising from children's television.'

HINTS

1 Prepare your case but don't write down more than a few bullet points. You need to think on your feet, respond to the opposition, and not be tied to a prepared script.
2 Aim to make two or three main points. Your partner – following the opposition speaker – should aim to repeat your points and then make two or three points of her/his own.
3 Remember that in a proper debate you can be challenged for points of information or questions from the opposition. You don't have to accept all of these, and in a five-minute speech you would be well advised to focus on two points on which to respond.

The audience should give you feedback on:
a) how you built up your case
b) clarity, pace, fluency, use of vocabulary and expression
c) how you dealt with points of information.

2. Polemical writing

Choose a topic you feel strongly about and write two polemical pieces – one for and one against. Aim to write approximately 250 words for each piece. Think through what the main arguments are and put them strongly and clearly (even if you are arguing for something you don't believe in).

Your topic could be:
- fox-hunting
- curfews on unruly youngsters
- not eating meat.

Aim to use:
- assertive language
- evidence, facts, statistics
- humour or anecdotes to entertain your reader.

3. Investigating the power of adverts

Investigate the effect of advertising on your class. Follow the steps below.
a) Choose one type of product (e.g. carbonated drinks, trainers, mobile phones).
b) Design a questionnaire, thinking carefully about your questions. You need to find out exactly why people buy which product and if they are influenced by adverts.
c) Undertake the research and analyse the results.
d) Present your findings in a written report. It should contain:
- an outline of how you approached the task
- how you built the questionnaire
- results
- commentary on what the results show
- any problems you encountered during the process.

ASSESS YOUR LEARNING

- Make significant contributions in discussions, evaluating others' ideas and varying how and when you participate
- Use vocabulary precisely and confidently to communicate clearly

a) How did you contribute during the various informal and formal discussions in this unit?

b) What ideas did other people express, and what did you think of them?

c) What feedback did you get from the audience of the debate?

d) What speaking and listening skills could you improve upon and how?

e) When you were speaking, did you ever struggle to find the right words? It is often helpful to jot down key words when preparing a speech, particularly specialist words which have a precise meaning.

• Show understanding of ways in which meaning and information are conveyed

• Identify and analyse argument, opinion and alternative interpretations

Use this continuum to track your progress with reading skills. Think back about how you responded to the texts in this unit.

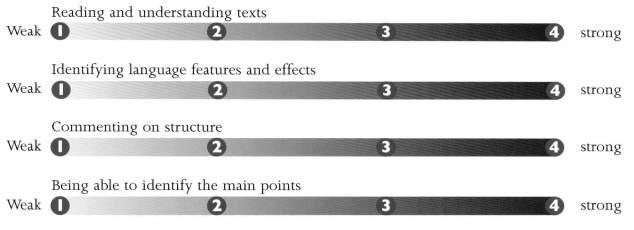

Reading and understanding texts

Weak ❶ ❷ ❸ ❹ strong

Identifying language features and effects

Weak ❶ ❷ ❸ ❹ strong

Commenting on structure

Weak ❶ ❷ ❸ ❹ strong

Being able to identify the main points

Weak ❶ ❷ ❸ ❹ strong

• Use grammatical features and vocabulary accurately and effectively

• Write non-fiction that is coherent and gives clear points of view

a) Check how the grammatical accuracy of your work is developing by comparing a piece of assessed work from this unit with one you completed several weeks or months ago. What developments do you notice?

b) Look at your polemic writing.

✦ How successful were you in organizing your ideas?

✦ What techniques are you developing to make your writing clear?

✦ How effectively can you express an opinion, without writing 'I think ...' too often?

FINISHING LINE

Imagine Martians have landed on earth. They have a phrasebook containing just 50 words in English. These words include:

1. **Here**
2. **No**
3. **Shop**
4. **Eat**
5. **Drink**
6. **Like**
7. **Move**
8. **Yesterday**
9. **Tomorrow**
10. **Friend**

Think of another 40 commonly used words in English (verbs as well as nouns) which you would find in a phrasebook. Then see how well you would be able to express the sentences at the bottom of the page in Martian language.

1. I am hungry. 2. I am going home tomorrow. 3. Where is the nearest shop? 4. The weather here feels cold. 5. At home I have many friends.

Learning objectives

By the end of this unit you should be able to:

- Choose structures, styles and registers of speaking and listening that are appropriate in a range of contexts
- Show confident use of standard English when required

- Select and combine a range of information from a variety of sources
- Sustain your responses to a demanding range of texts, developing your ideas and referring in detail to aspects of language, structure and presentation

- Use paragraphing and correct punctuation to make the sequence of events or ideas coherent
- Write, showing a selection of specific features to convey particular effects and to interest the reader

INTRODUCTION

This unit is about human beings – who we are, how others see us, and how we perceive ourselves and the outside world. These subjects are presented through a range of text types, such as biographies, essays and factual writing about body language.

(WARM-UP)

I Some people believe in horoscopes.
They say:

> Look at the way the moon affects the Earth – for example, in controlling tides. Since humans are more than 85% water, why shouldn't other planets have an influence over us?

Other people think horoscopes are nonsense. They say:

> Are we seriously expected to believe that the human race can be divided into 12 categories of personality? How do they explain that two friends of mine born on the same day are totally different?

With a partner, or in a small group, discuss these and your own views.

2 Read the quotations below. They are about character and personality.
   a) What do you understand by each one?
   b) Which do you agree with or like most?
   c) What do you understand by the expression 'a strong character'?
   d) How do you think character and personality are different?

I
Personality can open doors, but only character can keep them open.
                                    Elmer G. Letterman

II
The art of being yourself at your best is the art of unfolding your personality into the person you want to be … Be gentle with yourself, learn to love yourself, to forgive yourself, for only as we have the right attitude toward ourselves can we have the right attitude toward others.
                                    Wilfred Peterson

III
Nearly all men can stand adversity, but if you want to test a man's character, give him power.
                                    Abraham Lincoln

VI
A signature always reveals a man's character – and sometimes even his name.
                                    Evan Esar

V
People with courage and character always seem sinister to the rest.
                                    Hermann Hesse

3 We all present ourselves slightly differently when we are with different people. You may act and speak differently when you are with a parent from when you are with a best friend or group of friends; when you are with a teacher you may act differently from when you are alone.

If you play so many different roles with different audiences, which one is the 'real' you? Or do you think you are just a combination of different roles?

DIFFERENT PRESENTATIONS OF DICKENS

From around the seventeenth century, it became popular to keep diaries and journals. People wanted to look back over their lives, to reflect on the life they were living. In later centuries, biographies and autobiographies became fashionable. This section looks at how two different biographers have presented the Victorian novelist, Charles Dickens.

1 Before you read the texts, imagine you have been commissioned to write the biography of your headteacher. Brainstorm interesting ways of starting the biography, other than with his or her birth and childhood.

Now read the extracts below from biographies of Charles Dickens. Text A is from an early biography written by Dickens' friend, John Forster. Texts B, C, D and E are by a modern biographer, Peter Ackroyd. Ackroyd is himself a successful novelist and uses a number of different techniques to explore the life of Dickens – including unexpected starting-points and dialogue. Look out for these as you read.

TEXT A

CHAPTER I

CHARLES DICKENS, the most popular novelist of the century, and one of the greatest humorists that England has produced, was born at Landport, in Portsea, on Friday, the seventh of February, 1812.

His father, John Dickens, a clerk in the navy pay-office, was at this time stationed in the Portsmouth Dockyard. He had made acquaintance with the lady, Elizabeth Barrow, who became afterwards his wife, through her elder brother, Thomas Barrow, also engaged on the establishment at Somerset House; and she bore him in all a family of eight children, of whom two died in infancy. The eldest, Fanny (born 1810), was followed by Charles (entered in the baptismal register of Portsea as Charles John Huffham, though on the very rare occasions when he subscribed that name he wrote Huffam); by another son, named Alfred, who died in childhood; by Letitia (born 1816); by another daughter, Harriet, who died also in childhood; by Frederick (born 1820); by Alfred Lamert (born 1822); and by Augustus (born 1827).

From The Life of Charles Dickens by John Forster

TEXT B

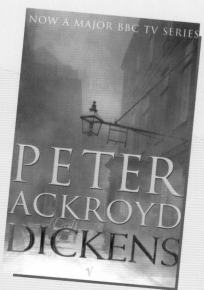

Prologue

CHARLES DICKENS was dead. He lay on a narrow green sofa – but there was room enough for him, so spare had he become – in the dining room of Gad's Hill Place. He had died in the house which he had first seen as a small boy and which his father had pointed out to him as a suitable object of his ambitions; so great was his father's hold upon his life that, forty years later, he had bought it. Now he had gone. It was customary to close the blinds and curtains, thus en-shrouding the corpse in darkness before its last journey to the tomb; but in the dining room of Gad's Hill the curtains were pulled apart and on this June day the bright sunshine streamed in, glittering on the large mirrors around the room. The family beside him knew how he enjoyed the light, how he needed the light; and they understood, too, that none of the conventional sombreness of the late Victorian period – the year was 1870 – had ever touched him.

From Dickens by Peter Ackroyd

Chapter 1

CHARLES DICKENS was born on the seventh of February 1812, the year of victory and the year of hardship. He came crying into the world in a small first-floor bedroom in an area known as New Town or Mile End, just on the outskirts of Portsmouth where his father, John Dickens, worked in the Navel Pay Office. His mother, Elizabeth, is reported to have claimed that she went to a ball on the night before his birth; but no ball is mentioned in the area for that particular evening and it is likely that this is one of the many apocryphal stories which sprung up around the birth and development of the great writer. He was born on a Friday, on the same day as his young hero David Copperfield, and for ever afterwards Friday became for him a day of omen. Whether like his young hero he was born just before midnight, when the tide was in, is not recorded; but this strange association between himself and his fictional characters is one that he carried with him always.

From *Dickens* by Peter Ackroyd

In this extract, Charles Dickens meets one of his own characters, *Little Dorrit*

BUT WHAT IF it were possible, after all, for Charles Dickens to enter one of his own novels? To bow his head and cross the threshold, into the world which he had created? And then meet Little Dorrit with her companion, the simpleton Maggie, as they walked slowly away from London Bridge in the darkest reaches of the night. Dickens was coming upon them when he heard the cry of the disturbed woman to Little Dorrit, "I never should have touched you, but I thought that you were a child." Then the woman hurried away, brushing against the sleeve of Dickens's coat; she gave him an agonised, fearful glance as once more she hid within the dark margins of the novel.

He did not look back at her, because he knew where she was going. He walked on towards Little Dorrit and, as he approached her, she looked up at him in alarm. "Pray do not be frightened," he whispered. "At all costs do not be frightened. I mean you no possible harm."

The quietness of his voice comforted her. "It is so dark, sir. And London is so barren and so wild."

"Those are my own sentiments, I assure you …" He was about to add something else, some further reassurance, but he checked himself. "Shall we walk on a little?" He offered Maggie his arm which she took with great aplomb (he still felt constrained with Little Dorrit) and, with the child of the Marshalsea beside them, they retraced their steps towards London Bridge. They stopped for a moment and looked down at the dark water flowing beneath them. "You know," he said, "I have often stood here as a boy. Telling stories to the small maid who once lived with us. Stories of the past. Stories of the future."

"And did they all come true, sir." Maggie asked. "Stories are meant to come true."

"Yes. They all came true." He looked at her curiously for a moment. "And I am telling stories still."

From *Dickens* by Peter Ackroyd

In the following extract, Peter Ackroyd meets Charles Dickens in a dream.

TEXT E

CHARLES DICKENS at the time of Peckwick, and of Oliver Twist, and of Nicholas Nickleby; the young man hurrying along, turning suddenly, looking up at the rolling clouds of a London sky, laughing at something in the street ahead of him. "Look at that! I have never been so surprised in all my life!"

"Tell me. Do please stay, and tell me where you are going."

"Where am I going? Where am I going? Why –" Dickens did stop for an instant, and scratched his head. "Why, that is a nice question. Oh Lord, yes. A very nice one." He saw a face moving past him, staring out of the window of an old-fashioned stage-coach, and he continued to watch it as the coach moved slowly down the street. Then he turned back, his span of attention as capacious and as impersonal as that of a cat. "I'll tell you where. I am going forward. I have been going forward ever since I began."

"Began?"

Two elderly women, fidgeting nervously as they talked to each other in loud voices, meandered past; Dickens watched them eagerly, restraining his urge to laugh out loud by compressing his lips together. Then, as soon as they had gone

by, he imitated their worried, puckered faces and their slightly nasal Cockney: "Vy, that one wos the commonest dirt, yes she wos." And then he carried on as if nothing whatever had happened. "Ever since I began the world." He stared fully at his questioner – straight at him, for a second or two, as if he were taking the measure of his entire life.

Before he turned around again, alerted by a voice raised suddenly in the pawnbroker's outside of which we were standing. A young woman came running out from the dilapidated shop (its wooden boards were damp and crumbling); Dickens stepped aside and let her pass, but looked at her so sharply that she felt the brightness of his glance upon her. She looked up at him as she ran off. "Did you see that face? I have never seen anything like it before! Truly, never!" But his questioner had seen only the startled appearance of a young woman caught by Dickens, as it were, while in pursuit of her own life. "What a fate she will have!" He murmured this with some satisfaction.

"Good day to you," he said abruptly. "I must be on my way."

From *Dickens* by Peter Ackroyd

2 Look again at Texts A and B. They were written more than 100 years apart.

   a) Draw up a grid, comparing the different styles of the two texts, looking at:
   - ✦ vocabulary/phrasing
   - ✦ tone
   - ✦ sentence structure
   - ✦ use of imagery
   - ✦ use of facts.

   b) Which text grabs your attention most and why?

3 In Texts D and E, Ackroyd uses some writing techniques that are often found in fiction rather than non-fiction. List the techniques that make the extracts feel like fiction. Your list might start like this:

- narrative with suspense
- use of imaginary characters
- description

4 One critic said this about Peter Ackroyd's biography:

> 'If a biography is any good, it will tell the story of a person's life without using gimmicks. The use of fictional techniques distracts us from the life of Dickens. It makes the biography as a whole feel less believable. We can't be sure what we can trust and what may be made up.'

In pairs, list some arguments for and against Peter Ackroyd's creative approach to biography.

You might consider aspects such as:
- ✦ factual content
- ✦ emotional appeal
- ✦ imaginative appeal
- ✦ accuracy.

WHO ARE WE?

 Many of us spend a lot of time worrying about who we really are, how we perceive the world and how people perceive us. Texts F and G explore how we present ourselves in public and what goes on inside our minds.

TEXT F

Face2Face

Nice to meet you

When you first meet someone, you have just 10 seconds to make an impression on them. Or to put it another way, the first 10 seconds after meeting a new person, you will be making a particular impression on them whether you like it or not.

Mind magic

Recent body language discoveries suggest that with a keen eye and ear, you can understand what people are thinking and how their minds work in very specific ways. According to psychologists, our bodytalk gives clues to how our brains are working. Quite simply, what we think about inside our heads, we express externally with our bodies.

As you probably know from your own experience, the people and experiences that we encounter in the outer world around us all have some inner association in our heads – perhaps in the form of a picture, a sound, or even a smell, taste or touch. (If you doubt that you do this, remember what colour the sheets are on your bed at the moment, or imagine what your favourite track would sound like played at half speed.) Everything we store in our brains has a representation there – even if we aren't able to see a totally vivid picture of it or hear a completely clear sound.

So, to interpret the bodytalk clues to what is going on in someone's head, begin with the simplest deduction: how is a person using their thought processes? Two American psychologists, Richard Bandler and John Grinder, have suggested that a person's eye movements show which sense they're thinking about – in other words, whether they're remembering or imagining something seen, heard, touched, smelled or tasted.

Bandler and Grinder suggest that if what a person is thinking about is something they have seen, they'll look up or defocus, sit up, raise their eyebrows, furrow their brow horizontally and breathe more quickly. If they're thinking about a sound, they'll look to the side, tilt their heads as if listening and breathe evenly. If what a person is thinking about is a feeling (either a sensation or an emotion) they'll look down and to the right, lean forward, round their shoulders, breathe deeply.

More specifically, if a person is remembering something that they *actually* saw or heard, their eyes will also slightly move to their left – but if they're imagining seeing or hearing something that hasn't actually happened yet, their eyes will move to their right. If they're thinking in words (what you might call "talking to themselves") then they'll look down and to their left, and often make tiny movements of throat or lips.

Each of these eye movements takes less than a fraction of a second; you may not even register them. They'll be strung together in sequences of several dozen, and so you can't possibly track every thought as it happens. But you can certainly get a great deal of information about whether someone typically thinks in pictures, words or feelings, and whether any one memory or creative thought is being experienced through any one particular sensory channel. Sometimes, with a clear signal, you can tell whether someone is remembering what they've seen, and ask, "What did they look like?", before they have told you their thought!

From *Body Language* by Susan Quilliam

TEXT G

Other Minds

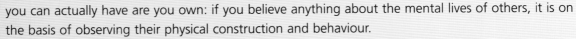

How much do you really know about what goes on in anyone else's mind? Clearly you observe only the bodies of other creatures, including people. You watch what they do, listen to what they say and to the other sounds they make, and see how they respond to their environment – what things attract them and what things repel them, what they eat, and so forth. You can also cut open other creatures and look at their physical insides, and perhaps compare their anatomy with yours.

But none of this will give you direct access to their experiences, thoughts, and feelings. The only experiences you can actually have are you own: if you believe anything about the mental lives of others, it is on the basis of observing their physical construction and behaviour.

To take a simple example, how do you know, when you and a friend are eating chocolate ice cream, whether it tastes the same to him as it tastes to you? You can try a taste of his ice cream, but if it tastes the same as yours, that only means it tastes the same *to you*: you haven't experienced the way it tastes *to him*. There seems to be no way to compare the two flavor experiences directly.

Well, you might say that since you're both human beings, and you can both distinguish among flavors of ice cream – for example you can both tell the difference between chocolate and vanilla with your eyes closed – it's likely that your flavor experiences are similar. But how do you know *that*? The only connection you've ever observed between a type of ice cream and a flavor is in your own case; so what reason do you have to think that similar correlations hold for other human beings? Why isn't it just as consistent with all the evidence that chocolate tastes to him the way vanilla tastes to you, and vice versa?

The same question could be asked about other kinds of experience. How do you know that red things don't look to your friend the way yellow things look to you? Of course it you ask him how a fire engine looks, he'll say it looks red, like blood, and not yellow, like a dandelion; but that's because he, like you, uses the word "red" for the color blood and fire engines look to him, *whatever* it is. Maybe it's what you call yellow, or what you call blue, or maybe it's a color experience you've even had, and can't even imagine.

From *What Does It All Mean?* by Thomas Nagel

ACTIVITIES

1 Text F looks at the way our body language communicates.
   a) Which parts did you find most interesting?
   b) Is there any of it that you don't agree with?

2 Imagine you want to investigate two people's body language when they are chatting. You want to see:
   - how far apart they stand
   - whether they face each other directly .
   - whether they make eye contact
   - what kind of gestures they make.

How might you set up the investigation so that you can observe them, but without them knowing what you are doing?

3 Look again at text G. Try to summarize its main message in one sentence.

4 Text G takes an abstract subject and aims to present it in a simple, easy-to-follow style.

a) On the graph below, plot how accessible (easy to understand) you find each paragraph.

b) Abstract concepts (such as ideas and perceptions) can sometimes be described in a complicated, scientific style. Write down three ways that the writer of Text G tries to make the material straightforward for the reader.

5 Texts F and G were both written for adult audiences. Yet they contain ideas that many younger people will find interesting.

a) Design an A4 leaflet for young people aged 11 to 14, presenting the ideas from one text. Use images and design features as well as text.

b) Sketch out your ideas and annotate the features showing how you have used design and language to make the subject matter accessible for the audience.

MY FACE

Text H is a complete essay written by drama critic and humorous writer, Robert Benchley. In it he looks at himself in the mirror ...

My Face

MERELY as an observer of natural phenomena, I am fascinated by my own personal appearance. This does not mean that I am pleased with it, mind you, or that I can even tolerate it. I simply have a morbid interest in it.

Each day I look like someone, or *something*, different. I never know what it is going to be until I steal a look in the glass. (Oh, I don't suppose you really could call it stealing. It belongs to me, after all.)

One day I look like Wimpy, the hamburger fancier in the Popeye the Sailor saga. Another day it may be Wallace Beery. And the third day, if I have let my mustache get out of hand, it is Bainsfather's Old Bill. And not until I peek do I know what the show is going to be.

Some mornings, if I look in the mirror soon enough after getting out of bed, there is no resemblance to any character at all, either in or out of fiction, and I turn quickly to look behind me, convinced that a stranger has spent the night with me and is peering over my shoulder in a sinister fashion, merely to frighten me. On such occasions, the shock of finding that I am actually possessor of the face in the mirror is sufficient to send me scurrying back to bed, completely unnerved.

All this is, of course, very depressing, and I often give off a low moan at the sight of the new day's metamorphosis, but I can't seem to resist the temptation to learn the worst. I even go out of my way to look at myself in store-window mirrors, just to see how long it will take me to recognize myself. If I happen to have on a new hat, or am walking with a limp, I sometimes pass right by my reflection without even nodding. Then I begin to think: "You must have given off *some* visual impression into that mirror. You're not a disembodied spirit yet – I hope!"

And I go back and look again, and, sure enough, the strange-looking man I thought was walking just ahead of me in the reflection turns out to have been my own image all the time. It makes a fellow stop and think, I can tell you.

This almost masochistic craving to offend my own aesthetic sense by looking at myself and wincing also comes out when snapshots or class photographs are being passed around. The minute someone brings the envelope containing the week's grist of vacation prints from the drugstore developing plant, I can hardly wait to get my hands on them. I try to dissemble my eagerness to examine those in which I myself figure, but there is a greedy look in my eye which must give me away.

The snapshots in which I do not appear are so much dross in my eyes, but I pretend that I am equally interested in them all.

"This is very good of Joe," I say, with a hollow ring to my voice, sneaking a look at the next print to see if I am in it.

Ah! Here, at last, is one in which I show up nicely. By "nicely" I mean "clearly." Try as I will to pass it by casually, my eyes rivet themselves on that corner of the group in which I am standing. And then, when the others have left the room, I surreptitiously go through the envelope again, just to gaze my fill on the slightly macabre sight of Myself as others see me.

In some pictures I look even worse than I had imagined. On what I call my "good days," I string along pretty close to form. But day in and day out, in mirror or in photograph, there is always that slight shock surprise which, although unpleasant, lends a tang to the adventure of peeking. I never can quite make it seem possible that that is really Poor Little Me, the Little Me I know so well and yet who frightens me so when face to face.

My only hope is that, in this constant metamorphosis which seems to be going on, a winning number may come up sometime, if only for a day. Just what the final outcome will be, it is hard to predict. I may settle down to a constant, plodding replica of Man-Mountain Dean in my old age, or change my style completely and end up as a series of Bulgarian peasant types. I may just grow old along with Wimpy.

But whatever is in store for me, I shall watch the daily modulations with an impersonal fascination not unmixed with awe at Mother Nature's gift for caricature, and will take the bitter with the sweet and keep a stiff upper lip.

As a matter of fact, my upper lip is pretty fascinating by itself, in a bizarre sort of way.

Glossary

Bainsfather's Old Bill – a portrait by painter Arthur Bainsfather

Man-Mountain Dean – an American wrestler of the 1920s and 30s

Wallace Beery – an American actor of the 1940s

Wimpy – a scruffy character in the famous Popeye comic book

From 'My Face' by Robert Benchley

ACTIVITIES

1 What impression do you get of Robert Benchley from the text? Use a spider diagram to note different aspects of his character.

2 Which of these words do you think best describes Benchley's style of writing in Text H: humorous, self-absorbed, ironic, poignant, complex.

3 The article was written more than 50 years ago.
a) What clues can you find that hint at its age?
b) Note any features that make it seem modern.

4 Look at yourself in a mirror. Think carefully about what you see and what your face reveals about you.

Write a paragraph describing your face and how you feel about it. You might want to start by describing the overall effect, or you might want to focus in on one detail to begin with. For example: 'Those nostrils are all wrong. They aren't supposed to look like that …'

UNIT CHALLENGES

1. Biography

Choose someone as a challenging subject for a biography. It should be an adult you know, such as your form teacher or a friend of your parents.

a) Interview your subject to find out details about his or her life (e.g. where they were born, their childhood, education and career).
b) Weave the facts into a compelling opening for a biography. Avoid a conventional opening like 'Mrs Miles was born in 1958 in Leicester …'. Instead, try a more original opening which would catch a reader's interest whilst giving genuine information about your subject. Here are some hints to get you started:

  ✦ Choose your subject carefully – someone who you will be able to spend some time interviewing.
  ✦ During the interview, make brief notes, but focus on the way this person looks and speaks – you might use these details in your opening sequence.
  ✦ Choose one key incident in your subject's life as the starting-point for your biography.
  ✦ Look at the way newspapers present profiles of people. For example, in the *Observer*, 12 September 2004, Paul Harris writes a profile of an American businessman. To get our attention, he begins like this:

'H. Lee Scott is the most important man you have never heard of. That won't be true for much longer…'

✦ Experiment with style. For example, see whether writing in the present or past tense has most impact; or decide whether to use the first person 'I' or keep the tone more impersonal.

2. Creative writing

Create a character who is going through an identity crisis. It might be someone who, on the surface, seems confident and is much admired, but who inwardly is insecure and worried. Think about how you might show the reader this without saying explicitly: 'Inside she felt worried'. Follow these steps:

✦ Decide on the form you wish to write in (e.g. a short story, the opening of a novel, a monologue).

✦ Spend time developing your character. Your starting point might be a name or place; think about your character's background or talents.

✦ Write an opening scene – an event or conflict during which your character's surface confidence is put under pressure, for example.

This is a demanding writing exercise. You may have to have several attempts before you get the opening right. You may wish to draft an opening, then give it to a partner for their response. Discuss the strengths and weaknesses. Aim to write a short, but concentrated, ambitious piece of character writing.

3. Vent your spleen

Select a topic, such as horoscopes, or a different issue that you have strong views about. Your challenge is to write an entertaining and provocative opinion piece that challenges your reader's views. If you think your reader believes that there is truth in horoscopes, aim to demonstrate categorically that it's all nonsense.

This is polemical journalism in the tradition of Julie Burchill and Will Self – writers who enjoy stirring up their readers. Aim to write something funny, slightly aggressive and definitely thought-provoking.

ASSESS YOUR LEARNING

● Choose structures, styles and registers of speaking and listening that are appropriate in a range of contexts

● Show confident use of standard English when required

Make a note of the different activities that involved speaking and listening in this unit (e.g. the warm-up discussion about horoscopes, the interview, discussing your draft work with a partner). Then jot down the style and tone you used. Consider:

✦ level of formality
✦ vocabulary
✦ use of different sentences types (e.g. imperatives, questions)

You should feel confident in using standard English in most situations. To show your understanding of what standard English is and when it is appropriate, think of some examples when you would NOT expect to use standard English.

● Select and combine a range of information from a variety of sources
● Sustain your responses to a demanding range of texts, developing your ideas and referring in detail to aspects of language, structure and presentation

a) What key ideas did you pick up from two of the texts in this unit?
b) Which texts in this unit did you find most challenging?
c) What strategies did you use when you came across concepts or vocabulary that you didn't understand?
d) What signs are there that you are better at noticing how a text is organized?
e) What signs are there that you are better at noticing features of vocabulary and sentences?

● Use paragraphing and correct punctuation to make the sequence of events or ideas coherent
● Write, showing a selection of specific features to convey particular effects and to interest the reader

a) Several pieces of writing in this unit require you to capture and then sustain the reader's attention. What kind of techniques have you learnt for this?
b) If someone asked your advice on how to make a boring subject interesting for a reader, what three hints would you give?

FINISHING LINE

Look at the cartoon. Think of some reasons why the man is smiling. Think of a caption, or some words that one of the characters might be saying.

Learning objectives

By the end of this unit you should be able to:

S
○ Take a leading role in discussions, listen with concentration and understanding
○ Show an assured and fluent use of standard English in a range of situations

R
○ Sustain responses to a demanding range of texts
○ Make apt and careful comparison between texts

W
○ Select specific features or expressions in your writing to convey effects
○ Write narrative which shows control of characters, events and settings, and variety in structure
○ Write non-fiction coherently, giving clear points of view
● Use vocabulary and grammar to make fine distinctions

INTRODUCTION

This unit looks at the ways texts from the past have shaped the texts that we read today – and why some of them are considered to be 'classics'.

WARM-UP

1 In a small group, discuss what makes a 'classic'. Use the statement and opinions below to trigger your ideas.

> IF SOMEONE SAYS TO ME THAT THEY PREFER WATCHING *NEIGHBOURS* TO WATCHING *MACBETH*, THAT'S FINE. BUT IF THEY SAY THAT *NEIGHBOURS* IS BETTER THAN *MACBETH*, I KNOW THE PERSON IS AN IDIOT.

> IT'S ARROGANT... BUT TRUE.

> IT'S NOT TRUE AT ALL. IF SOMEONE LIKES *NEIGHBOURS* MORE THAN *MACBETH*, THEN IT'S BETTER.

2 Look at the following list of films. Imagine you have been commissioned by a newspaper to write about the top five classic movies ever made.

2001: A SPACE ODYSSEY
AUSTIN POWERS
BRAVEHEART
BRIEF ENCOUNTER
CASABLANCA
DANCES WITH WOLVES
E.T.
FINDING NEMO
FORREST GUMP
GOOD WILL HUNTING
HARRY POTTER & THE PHILOSOPHER'S STONE
JAWS
LORD OF THE RINGS:
 THE FELLOWSHIP OF THE RING
MEN IN BLACK
RAIDERS OF THE LOST ARK
SCHINDLER'S LIST
SINGIN' IN THE RAIN
SOME LIKE IT HOT
STAR WARS
THE SIXTH SENSE
THE BIRDS
THE MATRIX
THE SHAWSHANK REDEMPTION
THE SOUND OF MUSIC
THE WIZARD OF OZ
TO KILL A MOCKINGBIRD

a) Discuss the list as a group. (You may not all know all the films.) Decide which films are the top five classics.
   ✦ You may choose films that are not on this list.
   ✦ You will need to decide what makes a 'classic' film (not necessarily the most popular).
b) Broaden out the discussion as to whether there are three key ingredients which make a classic, whether it is a movie, song, book or design.

TRADITIONAL TALES

This section explores the way history shapes storytelling. It includes superstitions, legends, myths and fairy tales.

ACTIVITY

I Look at the five definitions a to e on the next page, and decide which definition matches which word shown at the top of the page.

Fairy tale Superstition Legend Fable Myth

a) A story with a moral, usually with animals as characters.

b) An ancient story that deals with gods and heroes, especially one used to explain some natural phenomenon.

c) A traditional story which has popularly come to be regarded as true, but has not been confirmed as such.

d) Belief in an influence that certain (especially commonplace) objects, actions or occurrences have on events and people's lives.

e) A story for children about imaginary characters, fairies and magic.

 Now read Texts A to F, below. They are a mix of superstitions, poems, nursery rhymes, historical pieces and folk tales. Think about how these types of texts are used to entertain or instruct us.

TEXT A

Friday, beginning journey on

1804 C. SMITH *Conversations on Poetry* I 62. I knew another poor woman, who … made it a rule never to … set out on a journey on a Friday. **1855** *Gents Mag*. pt. 2 384 – 5 [Shrops. / Worcs.] Considered unlucky … to go a journey on a Friday. **1865** SURTEES *Mr Facey Romford's Hounds* LX. Friday is generally considered an unlucky day; at all events a day that people do not generally choose for their pleasure expeditions. **1890** MRS HENRY WOOD *Johnny Ludlow* 4th ser. 343 [Worcs.] We took the train at Evesham. It was Friday … Some people do not care to begin a journey on a Friday, thinking it bodes ill-luck: I might have thought the same had I foreseen what was to happen before we got home again. **1946** UTTLEY *Country Things* 128 [Cromford Derbys., *c.* 1900] Many people refused to start a journey on Friday, but Friday was market-day, and we took no notice of this.

From *A Dictionary of Superstitions*, edited by Iona Opie and Moira Tatem

TEXT B

THE ORIGINS OF GOOSEY GOOSEY GANDER

Goosey, goosey gander,
Whither shall I wander?
Upstairs and downstairs
And in my lady's chamber.
There I met an old man
Who would not say his prayers.
I took him by the left leg
And threw him down the stairs.

The earliest record of this rhyme does not embrace the last four lines, and it is very probable that they had a separate origin. They are much the same as the lines that schoolchildren address to the cranefly ('Daddy-long-legs'), sometimes pulling off its legs as they repeat,

> Old father Long-Legs
> Can't say his prayers:
> Take him by the left leg,
> And throw him downstairs.

A child who added the rhyme to his (or her) nursery rhyme book some 150 years ago seems to confirm the idea that two distinct pieces have been amalgamated:

> Goosey Goosey Gander where shall we wander
> Up stairs and down stairs and in my Lady's chamber.
> Old father long legs will not say his Prayers,
> Take him by the left leg and throw him downstairs.

It is certainly simpler to throw a cranefly downstairs than an old man. The earliest recording of the rhyme (1784) goes,

> Goose-a, goose-a, gander,
> Where shall I wander?
> Up stairs, down stairs,
> In my lady's chamber;
> There you'll find a cup of sack
> And a race of ginger.

In Hook's *Original Christmas Box* (1798) appears a verse:

> Up stairs, down stairs, upon my Lady's window
> There I saw a Cup of Sack, and a race of Ginger.
> Apples at the Fire and nuts to crack,
> A little Boy in the Cream Pot, up to his Neck.

It is possible that the original 'Goosey, goosey gander' rhyme was made up of these last two pieces.

From *Oxford Dictionary of Nursery Rhymes*, edited by Iona and Peter Opie

HISTORY OF KING CANUTE

CANUTE (Cnut) (d. 1086), king of Denmark and martyr, patron of Denmark … Canute became king of Denmark in 1081 in succession to his brother Harold. By now Denmark, largely evangelized by Englishmen, was nominally Christian: Canute promulgated laws which restrained the power of the *jarls* (or earls), protected the clergy, and exacted the payment of tithes for their upkeep, and in fact made some of them powerful temporal lords. He also built and endowed churches lavishly such as Lund. Roskilde (to which he gave his crown) became the burial place of Danish kings.

Twice he attempted unsuccessfully to invade England: first in 1075, when the three earls who rebelled against William the Conqueror asked for his help. His fleet of 200 ships achieved only a raid on York before the rebellion was suppressed. Again in 1085 Canute renewed his claim to the English throne, and started to assemble a huge fleet with his allies of Norway and Flanders. The threat was so serious that William the Conqueror imported numerous mercenaries, removed supplies from the coast, and soon instituted the famous Domesday Survey. In the event the attack came to nothing because Canute's subjects, led by the *jarls*, rebelled against his taxation, tithes, and 'new order', took his brother Olaf as their leader, and besieged Canute in the church of St. Alban at Odensee. After receiving the sacraments of Penance and the Eucharist, Canute was killed kneeling in front of the altar with eighteen followers.

From the *Oxford Dictionary of Saints*, edited by David Hugh Farmer

King Canute was weary-hearted; he had reigned for years a score,
Battling, struggling, pushing, fighting, killing much and robbing more;
And he thought upon his actions, walking by the wild seashore.

'Twixt the chancellor and bishop walked the king with steps sedate,
Chamberlains and grooms came after, silversticks and goldsticks great,
Chaplains, aides-de-camp, and pages – all the officers of state,

Sliding after like his shadow, pausing when he chose to pause:
If a frown his face contracted, straight the courtiers dropped their jaws;
If to laugh the king was minded, out they burst in loud heehaws.

But that day a something vexed him, that was clear to old and young:
Thrice his grace had yawned at table, when his favourite gleemen sung,
Once the queen would have consoled him, but he bade her hold her tongue.

'Something ails my gracious master,' cried the keeper of the seal.
'Sure, my lord, it is the lampreys served at dinner, or the veal?'
'Pshaw!' exclaimed the angry monarch. 'Keeper, 'tis not that I feel.

''Tis the heart, and not the dinner, fool, that doth my rest impair:
Can a king be great as I am, prithee, and yet know no care?
Oh, I'm sick, and tired, and weary.' – Someone cried, 'The king's arm-chair!'

Then towards the lackeys turning, quick my lord the keeper nodded,
Straight the king's great chair was brought him, by two footmen able-bodied;
Languidly he sank into it: it was comfortably wadded.

'Leading on my fierce companions,' cried he, 'over storm and brine,
I have fought and I have conquered! Where was glory like to mine?'
Loudly all the courtiers echoed: 'Where is glory like to thine?'

'Might I stay the sun above us, good sir Bishop?' Canute cried;
'Could I bid the silver moon to pause upon her heavenly ride?
If the moon obeys my orders, sure I can command the tide.

'Will the advancing waves obey me, bishop, if I make the sign?'
Said the bishop, bowing lowly, 'Land and sea, my lord, are thine.'
Canute turned towards the ocean – 'Back' he said, 'thou foaming brine.

'From the sacred shore I stand on, I command thee to retreat;
Venture not, thou stormy rebel, to approach thy master's seat:
Ocean, be thou still! I bid thee come not nearer to my feet!'

But the sullen ocean answered with a louder, deeper roar,
And the rapid waves drew nearer, falling sounding on the shore;
Back the keeper and the bishop, back the king and courtiers bore.

And he sternly bade them never more to kneel to human clay,
But alone to praise and worship That which earth and seas obey:
And his golden crown of empire never wore he from that day.
… King Canute is dead and gone: parasites exist alway.

Glossary
brine – salt water
gleemen – musicians
lampreys – eel-like fish

From 'King Canute' by William Makepeace Thackeray

The Baker's Daughter

The baker was thin-lipped; he never gave as much as a crumb away. But his daughter was worse. Not only was she mean; she simpered and toadied to the rich and insulted and sniffed at the poor.

At dusk one of the good people came walking by. She picked up some old clothes that had long served their mistress and been left out for the rag-and-bone man; she slipped them on. She pressed her palms against the dusty face of the street and rubbed her cheeks.

Then the woman dragged herself into the baker's shop. The baker was out and his daughter looked at the woman and tossed back her fair hair. "Yes?" she said.

"Can you spare me some dough?" said the woman.

"Dough?" said the girl. "Why should I? If I give dough to everyone who comes through that door, there won't be any left, will there?"

The woman hung her head. "…haven't any money," she mumbled.

"Whose fault is that?" asked the girl.

"….anything to eat."

"Eh?" said the girl, pulling a small piece of dough off the floury, flabby mound that wallowed on the table behind her. "Think yourself lucky!" she said, and she shoved the piece into the oven on the rack just beneath her own trays of well-shaped loaves.

When the girl opened the oven again, she saw that the woman's dough had so risen that she had the biggest loaf in the oven.

"I'm not giving you that," said the girl, "If that's what you think."

She twisted off another piece of dough, no more than half the size of the small first piece. "You'll have to wait," said the girl, and she shoved it into the oven under another batch of her own loaves.

But this piece of dough swelled even more than the first piece, and the second loaf was larger than the first loaf.

"Or that!" exclaimed the girl. "Certainly not!"

The baker's daughter tossed back her hair in a temper and squeezed off a third piece of dough scarcely bigger than your thumb. She shoved that into the oven under a batch of a fairy cakes, and slammed the door.

After a while, the girl turned round to open the oven again. Behind her, meanwhile, the woman slipped off her ragged clothing. She stood in the baker's shop, tall and white and shining.

When the girl opened the oven, she saw that the third piece of dough had so risen that it was the biggest loaf of all three.

The girl stared at the loaf. Her eyes opened, very round and very wide. "Why," she said, turning round to face the beggar woman, "why, who, who …"

"Whoo-whoo!" cried the good woman. "Whoo-whoo! That's all you'll ever say again."

The girl cowered on the other side of the counter.

"Whoo-whoo!" cried the woman. "This world's put up with you for long enough – you and your sniffs and insults." Then she raised her stick and struck the girl's right shoulder with it.

At once the baker's daughter turned into an owl. She flew straight out of the door, hooting, and away into the dark reaches of the night.

From *British Folk Tales* by Kevin Crossley-Holland

2 Look again at Text A.

a) Have you come across any superstitions about Fridays before? If so, what are they?

b) What superstitions do you know from your own family (parents and grandparents)? Many superstitions are about the moon, cats, frogs, items of clothing, colours and household items such as umbrellas, mirrors and shoes.

c) Why do you think people in the past might have been more superstitious than we think we are?

3 Look at Text B.

a) Which ideas interest you and why?

b) Does anything surprise you or seem silly?

c) Think about any morals or messages the following nursery rhymes might contain. For example, with Wee Willy Winkie you might say: 'This shows that the idea of child curfews isn't new. Wee Willie Winkie wanders the town to make sure all children are safely in their homes. This is an early attempt to crack down on anti-social behaviour.'

Wee Willy Winkie	Jack and Jill
Little Jack Horner	Simple Simon

d) Do some research into the origins of a nursery rhyme. Then produce a fact sheet or poster containing your findings.

Some good sources of information are:
- Iona and Peter Opie, the *Oxford Dictionary of Nursery Rhymes*
- www.rhymes.org.uk
- www.sca.org.au/bacchus_wood/origins_of_nursery_rhymes.html
- www.indianchild.com/history_origins_nursery_rhymes.html

4 Look at Texts C and D. Both are about King Canute. One is a short historical extract; the other is a poem written by the Victorian writer, William Makepeace Thackeray. Use the prompts in the grid below to compare the texts.

	Text C	Text D
1 List three main facts you learnt about Canute.		
2 What impression do you get of the character of Canute?		
3 What do we learn from Text D which we don't learn from Text C?		
4 Which text did you enjoy more and why?		

5 Experiment with writing texts in different forms.
  a) Try writing Text C in the form of a poem, and Text D in the form of a factual text (in a continuous paragraph).
  b) Can you still tell what genres (text types they are)? If so, how?

6 Text E is a traditional English folk-tale retold by Kevin Crossley-Holland. In what ways does it feel like a folk-tale rather than a modern novel? Look for clues in the content and the language of the story.

7 Imagine the baker's daughter feels she has been badly misrepresented by this story. The reality of her situation, she feels, was very different. Write the opening of a monologue in which she puts her point of view. Imagine a setting where she sits and addresses a camera, telling us why things aren't the way they appear in the story. You might start like this:

> Didn't anyone ever tell you not to believe everything you read? It's fine to read fiction, but just don't confuse it with fact. The way I'm presented in that story – he doesn't even have the courtesy to give me a name – is a lie, pure and simple. So let's put the record straight ...

FOOD FOR THOUGHT

The theme of this section is cooking, but before you read the main texts, think about what you expect from a good cookery book.

ACTIVITY

1 Which of the elements listed below do you think are most and least important in a cookery book? Use a continuum like the one below to record your decisions.

Most important ———————————————▶ least important

  ✦ Clear instructions
  ✦ Step-by-step instructions
  ✦ Lively authorial style
  ✦ Background information about ingredients
  ✦ Teaching techniques for cooking properly
  ✦ Written with a passion for food
  ✦ Lots of photographs or diagrams
  ✦ Short paragraphs
  ✦ Straightforward vocabulary

Now read the three non-fiction texts that follow, all of which focus on cooking. The first is an extract from a classic Victorian cookery book; the second is by Nigel Slater who writes about bread-making; the last text is advice on how to make toast by one of Britain's best-known cookery writers, Delia Smith.

As you read, think about what the texts reveal about the authors, the period in which they were written and the language of the time, as well as the information about food itself.

BREAD, ROLLS, BUNS, BISCUITS, &c.

Bread is a principal part of the food of persons in all conditions of life, it is therefore of the first importance that it should be good. This depends on several circumstances. 1. The goodness of the corn, which must be well grown, free from blight and mildew, favourably gathered in its proper season, and used while its goodness remains unimpaired. If corn be suffered to remain too long on the ground by reason of wet weather, or if it be exposed to rain after it is cut, the grain begins to germinate, and the flour and bread procured from such grain is clammy and unwholesome. Grain, well housed and securely kept, will remain sound and good for a long time. This is a merciful provision by which the surplus of one year is available to meet the deficiencies of another; but it was never intended that grain should be hoarded year after year for the purposes of pride, covetousness, and oppression; nor can such speculations be practised without injury to the grain and its consumers; and not unfrequently to the covetousness withholders of it also. 2. The flour should also be used within a proper time after grinding. It may with advantage be kept four or five weeks, but should not exceed six. Exposure to the air causes it to evaporate and lose some of its nutritious properties; and if it becomes at all damp, fermentation and acidity take place. Flour should therefore be kept in a dry place and covered up to secure it both from air and dust. 3. The admission of any foreign mixtures is to be highly depreciated. When bread is sold at a standard weight and price, it is a great temptation to bakers to adulterate their bread with inferior, and perhaps pernicious articles; or at least to use such things in the process of making bread as will cause it to rise quickly and retain its moisture and weight, as well as add to its whiteness: among the least pernicious of these are alum and pearl ash, and even these are very disagreeable. It is much to be desired that a free competition were allowed in the preparation of this most important article of food; thus the honest baker would be encouraged and the public benefitted.

From *The New London Cookery and Complete Domestic Guide* by a Lady

TEXT G

There is something that annoys me about people who say they always bake their own bread. It's not just that it is virtually impossible to make such a claim without sounding ever so slightly smug, nor is it that it reminds me that the state of suppressed chaos I live in forbids such good housekeeping. I suspect it is simply that I know what I am missing. That wonderful buzz, albeit a slightly self-righteous one in my case, that you get when you take your own loaf from the oven.

I do bake my own bread as it happens. At least once a year. And always in the spring. No doubt it has something to do with some primeval force, the same one that makes me lust for long walks in the countryside or steers me towards the garden centre. In the past I have toyed with rich golden brioche, slaved over politically correct organic wholemeal loaves and even amused myself with fruit-laden German Stollen.

Focaccia, the excruciatingly fashionable Italian bread, has been baked since before there were ovens. It is a hearth-bread, cooked for thousands of years on flat stones in the hearth, covered by hot ashes. The name comes from focus, the Latin for hearth, the focus or hub of the household. I shall not attempt one of these ashbreads in my hearth. I lack the thick schiacce, the flat rough stone kept in the embers that gives rise to schiacciate, the Tuscan name for focaccia. And I am not sure what my Coalite is actually made from.

I am slightly suspicious of the 3-inch-thick slabs of focaccia on sale at the moment. Can this somewhat cake-like bread, topped with herbs and sun-dried tomatoes and rich with extra virgin oil, be true to its name? A rather grand version I am sure. I want mine to be the epitome of a true Ligurian country hearth-bread, baked in the embers – or as near as I can get in a 1990s designer oven.

Making the dough is reassuringly simple. The yeast is thrown in with the flour, mixed with warm water and olive oil, then pummelled about a bit. After an hour of being ignored, the dough rises dutifully and is ready to be bashed about again and baked. It is as simple as that.

The real joy is the kneading. I love the feel of the warm dough in my hands. It is soft and warm yes, but it is also alive. The warm water and flour goad the yeast into producing the carbon dioxide that makes the dough rise, literally making it come to life. On the table, which is covered in flour, I continue stretching the dough and gathering it back into a ball until it softens. In the space of 10 minutes my tense ball of dough has become soft, springy and relaxed. It has come to life.

158

From *Real Good Food* by Nigel Slater

Focaccia Bread

Toast

A friend of mine invented the term 'wangy', a very accurate word to describe what 90 per cent of the world's catering establishments call toast. It's a good word because we're all absolutely familiar with what it's saying – cold, leathery, bendy little triangles that arrive at breakfast when you are asked, 'Would you like some toast?'

So I've been thinking, as this is a basic cookery course, why not give the world the definitive recipe for perfect toast? To begin with, I am not a disciple of automatic toasters. The ones I've experienced all seem to be a bit hit and miss, and if you're rather inept at slicing the bread (like me), then they're not very helpful at all because if the bread is slightly wonky, a) it probably won't go in the toaster at all, and b) if it does, one bit ends up not being toasted at all while the other bit is giving off nasty black smoke signals!

1. The key to slicing bread is to use gentle, rapid sawing movements with the knife and not to push down too hard on the loaf. For toast, cut the bread into slice of about $\frac{1}{2}$ inch (1 cm) thickness. The crusts can be on or off, depending on how you like them.
2. Pre-heat the grill for at least 10 minutes before making the toast, turning it to its highest setting.
3. Place the bread on the grill rack and position the tray 2 inches (5 cm) from the heat source.
4. Allow the bread to toast on both sides to your own preferred degree of pale or dark golden brown.
5. While that is happening, keep an eye on it and don't wander far away.
6. When the toast is done, remove it immediately to a toast rack. Why a toast rack? Because they are a brilliant invention. Freshly made toast contains steam, and if you place it in a vertical position, in which the air is allowed to circulate, the steam escapes and the toast becomes crisp and crunchy. Putting it straight on to a plate means the steam is trapped underneath, making it damp and soggy. If you don't possess a toast rack you really ought to invest in a modest one. Failing that, stand your slices of toast up against a jar or something similar for about 1 minute before serving.
7. Always eat toast as soon as possible after that, and never make it ahead of time.
8. Never ever wrap it in a napkin or cover it (the cardinal sin of the catering trade), because the steam gets trapped and the toast gets soggy.
9. Always use good bread, because the better the bread, the better the toast. It is also preferable if the bread is a couple of days old.

From How to Cook, Book 1 by Delia Smith

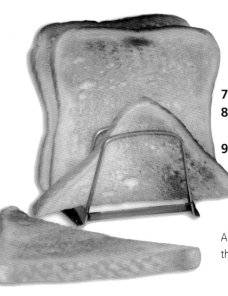

A toast rack is absolutely necessary if you want to avoid soggy toast; failing that, prop the slices up against a jar for a minute or so before serving.

ACTIVITIES

2 Compare the three texts. In particular, look closely at the authors' use of language. Copy and complete the grid below. Remember to give examples from the texts to back up your opinions.

	Text F	Text G	Text H
AUDIENCE: Who do you think the text is written for? ▶ Is the audience general or specialist? ▶ What age group or gender? ▶ Does the author address them as friends, acquaintances, strangers?			
PURPOSE: What do you think the text is aiming to achieve? ▶ To entertain, persuade, instruct, inform? ▶ How can you tell? ▶ Is it instructing us precisely how to do things, or giving us general information?			
FORM: What can you tell about when the text was written? ▶ Is it modern or historical? ▶ How can you tell? ▶ How is the text set out? ▶ How does the writer use words, sentences, paragraphs, layout features, such as headings, subheadings, capitals, bullet points, spacing?			

3 Text F was written around 150 years ago.
a) With a partner, talk about how it might be written if it was being published today.
b) Rewrite one paragraph in a more modern style.
c) Annotate your text, using arrows and labels to show the main changes you have made in order to update the text.

4 In Text H, Delia Smith teaches us how to make toast. Imagine you have just 50 words to teach someone how to make the perfect cup of tea. Draft and revise some instructions. Remember every word counts!

5 Look more closely at Text G. Nigel Slater's style does not feel like a typical piece of cookery writing. Write a paragraph describing his writing style. You might mention:
  - ✦ the way he refers to himself
  - ✦ his use of descriptive language
  - ✦ his choice of vocabulary
  - ✦ the style and length of his sentences and paragraphs
  - ✦ the structure of his writing
  - ✦ the use of humour, metaphors, similes, hyperbole (deliberate exaggeration).

THE MONSTER

In his novel *Star of the Sea*, Joseph O'Connor recreates the language and structure of a Victorian novel. His book is a murder mystery set upon a ship that is transporting passengers from the Irish famine in the nineteenth century to a promised new world in America.

As you read the opening pages of Text I, think carefully about how the author grabs the readers' attention from the start.

The Monster

A preface; in which are sketched certain recollections of THE STAR OF THE SEA; the condition of her passengers and the evil which stalked among them.

All night long he would walk the ship, from bow to stern, from dusk until quarterlight, that sticklike limping man from Connemara with the drooping shoulders and ash-coloured clothes.

The sailors, the watchmen, the lurkers near the wheelhouse would glance from their conversations or their solitary work and see him shifting through the vaporous darkness; cautiously, furtively, always alone, his left foot dragging as though hefting an anchor. A billycock hat was crumpled on his head, a ragged scarf wound around his chin and throat; his tattered military greatcoat so utterly dirty it was impossible to imagine it ever having been clean.

He moved with a deliberation that was almost ceremonial, a curious strain of threadbare stateliness: as a king in a story in disguise among his lessers. His arms were very long, his eyes needle-bright. Frequently he had a look of bewilderment or foreboding, as though his life had come to a point that was beyond explication or was drawing ever closer to such a point now.

His mournful face was disfigured with scars, cross-hatched with the blemishes of some affliction much exacerbated by his bouts of furious scratching. Though slender in build, made like a featherweight, he seemed to carry an indescribable burden. Neither was it a matter of his deformity alone — a distorted foot in a brick of a wooden clog which was stamped or branded with a capital M — but the air of anguished expectancy he bore; the perpetually frightened watchfulness of the abused child.

He was one of those men who attract great attention by making a great effort to attract none. Often, although they could not explain it, the sailors had a sense of his presence before seeing him. It became their amusement to wager on his whereabouts at a given hour. 'Ten bells' meant down by the starboard pigpens. Quarter after eleven found him up at the scuttlebutt where by day the destitute women of steerage prepared what little food they had — but even by the third night out of Liverpool the contest had lost its power to kill the time. He walked the ship as though following a rite. Up. Down. Across. Back. Stem. Port. Stern. Starboard. Materialising with the stars, stealing below with the sunrise, he came to be known among the ship's nocturnal denizens as 'the Ghost'.

Never did he engage the sailors in conversation. The night-stragglers, also, he completely eschewed. Not even after midnight would he speak to another, when anyone still above boards would talk to anyone else; when the dark, wet deck of the *Star of the Sea* saw a fellowship seldom apparent by daylight. Gates were left open at night on the ship; rules relaxed or quite ignored. It was illusory, of course, this witching hour democracy; darkness seeming to obliterate station or creed, or at least level them down to a point where they were not worth acknowledging. An acknowledgement in itself, perhaps, of the axiomatic powerlessness of being at sea.

At night one sensed the ship as absurdly out of its elements, a creaking, leaking, incompetent concoction of oak and pitch and nails and faith, bobbing on a wilderness of viciously black water which could explode at the slightest provocation. People spoke quietly on the decks after dark, as though fearful of awakening the ocean to savagery. Or one pictured the *Star* as a colossal beast of burden, its rib-timbers straining as though they might burst; flailed by an overlord into one last persecution, the hulk half dead already and we passengers its parasites. But the metaphor is not a good one for not all of us were parasites. Those of us who were would not have admitted it.

Below us the depths which could only be imagined, the gorges and canyons of that unfathomed continent: above us the death-black bowl of the sky. Wind pounded down in an outrage of screams from what even the most sceptical mariner was careful to term 'the heavens'. And the breakers thrashed and battered our shelter; like wind made flesh, incarnate and animate, a derision of the hubris of those who had dared to invade them. Yet there was an all but religious tranquillity among those who walked the decks at night: the angrier the sea, the icier the rain, the more palpable the solidarity among those withstanding them together. An admiral might chat to a frightened cabin boy, a hungry man of steerage to a sleepless Earl. One night a prisoner, a maddened violent Galwayman, was brought from the lock-up to take his doleful exercise. Even he was included in this communion of the somnambulant, quietly conversing and sharing a cup of rum with a Methodist minister from Lyme Regis in England who had never tasted rum before but had often preached its evils. (Together they were observed kneeling on the quarterdeck and quietly singing 'Abide With Me'.)

New things were possible in this Republic of night-time. But the Ghost showed no interest in possibility, or novelty. He was immune; a crag in the vastness surrounding him. Prometheus in rags, awaiting the avid birds. He stood by the mainmast watching the Atlantic as though expecting it to freeze over or bubble with blood.

Between first bell and two bells most would slip away; many alone but some together, for tolerances flowered under night's kind cover; nature and loneliness bedfellows in the dark. From three until first light, little happened on deck. It rose and it fell. It climbed. It plunged. Even the animals slept in their cages: pigs and chickens, sheep and geese. The clang of the watch-bell would sometimes puncture the ceaseless and numbing susurration of the sea. A sailor might sing shanties to keep himself awake: he and a comrade might tell stories to each other. From down in the lock-up the madman was intermittently heard, yelping like a wounded dog or threatening to brain the other prisoner with a handspike. (There was, at that time, no other prisoner.) A couple might be glimpsed in the shadowed alleyway formed by the aft wall of the wheelhouse and the base of the funnel. Still he would stand, that man from Connemara, gazing out at the awesome darkness; facing like a figurehead into the sleet, until the webs of the rigging emerged from the murk, so black against the reddening sky of dawn.

From *Star of the Sea* by Joseph O'Connor

Glossary
Billycock hat – a kind of bowler hat
Connemara – barren coastal region of western Ireland
Methodist – a member of the Methodist church who rejects the drinking of alcohol
Prometheus – in Greek mythology, Prometheus dared to steal fire from the gods. As punishment he was chained to a mountain and his liver pecked out by an eagle – a process that was repeated each day

ACTIVITIES

1 How does the writer create the world of the past? Think about how he presents this opening sequence, as well as what happens in the story.

2 What picture do you build up of the central character, 'the monster'? Draw a quick sketch of him, labelling it with the details from the story.

3 Find five examples of description that make the central character mysterious and sinister. Against each example, explain its effect.

Quotation	Why it makes the character seem mysterious and sinister

UNIT CHALLENGES

1. Narrative

Like the extract from *Star of the Sea*, write your own opening to a historical novel.

a) Choose a period that you are interested in, then a vivid, atmospheric setting. For example:
   ✦ a murky backstreet in Victorian London
   ✦ a vibrant theatre in Elizabethan England
   ✦ the dangerous interior of an air-raid shelter in the Second World War.

b) Choose a character and start to build an opening scene.

c) Experiment with time and point of view. You might have two voices, one in the present tense, one in the past, and alternate their narratives, like this:

'I watch as the crowd arrives and then I see you take your seat, smiling and contented, unaware of me watching you ...'

'The clouds were threatening rain as Mary finally found her way into the balcony over the groundlings' heads ...'

d) Write a creative, adventurous story opening that experiments with interesting storytelling techniques.

e) When you are satisfied with your story opening, write a one-paragraph commentary reflecting on the approaches you have used.

2. Chairing a discussion

Organize a discussion, like those on television news or arts programmes.
a) Get together three or four people from your class.

b) Tell them that the topic is 'the most influential products or achievements of the past 100 years'. The aim of the discussion is to provoke debate about how we judge what has made the most impact on our lives.

c) Each participant should argue for one item and has two minutes to make their case.

Here are some possible products:

- ✦ the iPod
- ✦ the Sony Walkman
- ✦ supersonic flight
- ✦ the laptop computer
- ✦ IKEA

- ✦ the personal computer
- ✦ the Mini
- ✦ the Internet
- ✦ satellite television
- ✦ electronic tagging of prisoners

Your role is to introduce the speakers, give them air-time, and encourage calm, controlled discussion. At the end you will invite your audience to vote on the most influential product.

Think about:

- ✦ How you will introduce the discussion
- ✦ How you will encourage everyone to have their say
- ✦ How you will deal with people who either dominate or don't say much
- ✦ How you will draw the debate to a conclusion.

3. Non-fiction writing

Think of something you are an expert in – it might be knowledge of a particular sport or type of music; it might be a hobby (such as wind-surfing or ten-pin bowling). Based on the non-fiction texts you have read in this unit, put together a short guide (one side of A4 paper) to the topic. Include:

- ✦ instructions and guidance
- ✦ opinions from different viewpoints (e.g. various experts giving their advice on the topic)
- ✦ images/diagrams that help to explain the topic.

Imagine your fact sheet is aimed at a general, rather than a specialist audience. You are introducing them to the topic. Your work needs to be authoritative and yet reassuring.

a) Think carefully about how you will present the information.

b) Do your research.

c) Make your first draft. You may wish to show it to a partner for his or her feedback.

d) Finalize your work, checking the detail and its presentation.

ASSESS YOUR LEARNING

- Take a leading role in discussions, listen with concentration and understanding
- Show an assured and fluent use of standard English in a range of situations

Assess your role in the various discussions throughout this unit.
Give yourself marks out of ten for:

- ✦ regularly and confidently using standard English
- ✦ switching from formal to informal situations with ease
- ✦ adjusting your language for different purposes and audiences.

In chairing the 'products and designs' debate:

- ✦ How did you organize the discussion?
- ✦ What were your strengths and weaknesses?
- ✦ What feedback did you get from others?

Note down which areas of your spoken English you now need to develop.

- Sustain responses to a demanding range of texts
- Make apt and careful comparison between texts

a) Use spider diagrams to record the range of texts you have covered in this unit, and their main features.

b) On a scale of 1 (low) to 5 (high), how easy did you find it to comment on the comparison of audience, purpose and form when considering Texts F, G and H?

- Select specific features or expressions in your writing to convey effects
- Write narrative that shows control of characters, events and settings, and variety in structure
- Write non-fiction coherently, giving clear points of view
- Use vocabulary and grammar to make fine distinctions

a) Write a brief paragraph about the development of your narrative writing. Include:

- ✦ what shows innovation and a deliberate attempt to catch the reader's interest
- ✦ how you use tense, point of view, and other narrative techniques.

b) Write another paragraph about the development of your non-fiction writing. Include:
  ✦ what you found easy and difficult about putting together an information sheet
  ✦ how you ensured that different views were included.

FINISHING LINE

This unit looks at the concept of classics. Choose one topic below and name what you think are the top three classics.
  ✦ books for children
  ✦ television music shows
  ✦ situation comedies
  ✦ cartoons
  ✦ animated movies.

Justify your choices.

This unit is designed to help you excel in the reading and writing sections of the Key Stage 3 English Tests. It contains essential information, tips for success, and small practice exercises to enable you to monitor your progress.

Learning objectives

● Understand the requirements of the reading sections of the Key Stage 3 tests
● Know your own strengths and weaknesses in reading and writing
● Build your reading and writing skills in preparation for the tests
● Understand how to achieve a high level

KNOW THE PAPERS

To prepare yourself for the Key Stage 3 test, you need to know the format of the papers. Read through the Test briefing below.

(TEST BRIEFING)

The Key Stage 3 English test consists of three papers: Reading, Writing, and Shakespeare. Read the summary of the three papers in the grid below. Give yourself no more than five minutes to absorb the information.

Reading

✦ The Reading paper lasts 75 minutes, including 15 minutes' reading time.
✦ It consists of a reading booklet containing three texts and a reading answer booklet that contains approximately 15 questions. The questions are varied in format and worth between 1 and 5 marks.
✦ The three texts in the reading booklet will be varied, i.e. literary, non-literary, fiction and non-fiction.
✦ The format of the questions in the answer booklet indicates how many points are to be made and the amount that is to be written.

Writing

✦ The Writing paper is 75 minutes long. It comprises a longer task (45 minutes, including 15 minutes' recommended planning time) and a shorter task (30 minutes).

Main features of the longer writing task

✦ The task carries 30 marks.
✦ The task is supported by information about audience, form, purpose and how formal it should be.
✦ A planning format is provided.

Main features of the shorter writing task

✦ The task carries 20 marks, including 4 marks for spelling.
✦ No planning format is provided but there is information about structure, audience and purpose.

Shakespeare

✦ The Shakespeare reading task lasts 45 minutes. It is based on the detailed study of two sections set from one of three Shakespeare plays.
✦ The task focuses on two extracts from the set sections, which will be printed on the paper, and you will be asked to write a detailed response drawing on both extracts.
✦ Each task focuses on one of the four areas for assessment:
 – character and motivation
 – language of the text
 – ideas, themes and issues
 – text in the performance
✦ The task is assessed only for understanding and response to the play – not for written expression.

With a partner, or in a small group, choose one of the following activities to reinforce your knowledge of the test papers:

168

1   Quick-fire test questions:
    a) How many different papers will you sit?
    b) How will you be assessed on your knowledge of Shakespeare?
    c) How many extracts will you be tested on?
    d) How long is the Reading paper?
    e) How will the shorter and longer writing tasks be different?

2   Design a memorable, highly visual poster which summarizes the main ingredients of each paper. Display it in your classroom.

3   Design and print out a bookmark which contains essential information about the test format.

READING PAPER

The first challenge of the reading paper is the amount that you will need to read in the 15 minutes' reading time. The booklet contains a lot of material. This book, *English Challenge*, has been designed to give you plenty of practice in reading and comparing a wide range of texts. Think carefully about your answers to the following questions:

1   In 15 minutes' reading time, how would you approach the need to read three texts? Would you:
    ✦   spend five minutes on each text, whatever its length
    ✦   make notes
    ✦   annotate the texts
    ✦   look for key words
    ✦   skim-read
    ✦   read in depth?

2   Practise reading extracts in timed conditions. Are you confident about identifying key information quickly?

REMEMBER

The questions may ask you to:
✦   complete a table or tick box
✦   find, explain, and analyse textual details
✦   give short answers in your own words
✦   give long answers in your own words.

Questions may be asked at:
✦   word level (comment on the writer's use of a word)
✦   sentence level (comment on the writer's use of a sentence)
✦   text level (comment on the overall structure or tone of a text).

Your teacher will be able to give you closer guidance on the exact Attainment Targets required for each level of response.

QUESTION-SETTING PRACTICE

Look at the text below. It is an extract from a travel book by Vivienne de Watteville in which the author describes being chased by rhinoceroses.

Working in pairs or a small group, think of questions you might be asked about the text. This activity should help you to understand the importance of reading the detail of the text.

HINTS

✦ Aim to ask something at word, sentence and text level.
✦ Explore the structure and tone of the text and, perhaps, the character of the narrator, the historical or cultural setting, what might happen next.
✦ Aim to include the range of question types listed in the Reading section.
✦ In setting each question, think carefully about the opportunity you are giving your reader to display his or her abilities:
  - How will you recognize a good answer?
  - How will you encourage exceptional readers to show their knowledge and understanding?
  - How will you help them to focus on the language of the text, which is one of the main features of high-level responses?

Amongst the Rhinos

Before I had time to skip out of his sight he had made up his mind to charge me. The angry thunder of his snort, mingled with a screech like an engine blowing off steam, lent me wings. When I dared throw a glance over my shoulder I saw that both rhino were bearing down upon me with frightening speed. The boys had had a start of me, and as I raced after them across the vistas of stone bare as asphalt without a blade of cover anywhere, conviction swept over me that this time the game was up.

Though I ran and ran as I have never run in my life before, and my heart pounded in my ears and my lungs stiffened with the pain of drawing breath, time went suddenly into slow motion. Each step was weighted with lead; I wanted to fly over the ground and, as in some horrid nightmare, I felt as though I were scarcely moving.

The rhino were swiftly gaining upon me; their furious snorts overtook me on the wings of the gale. The boys, on the other hand, had disappeared as though the earth had swallowed them. I made one more desperate spurt and then, as I realised the utter futility of it, a fold in the hillside opened to receive me also. I tumbled headlong down a little cliff and landed on a ledge of heather.

The rhino would never face this drop even if they looked over and saw me. I glanced up apprehensively, but there was no sign of them.

In this sheltered place there was not a sound, and even the wind had dropped. With a thankful heart I stretched myself face downward on the heather, and panted as though I could never get a complete lungful of air again, while waves of crimson and orange rushed and throbbed before my eyes.

From *Speak to the Earth: Wanderings and Reflections among Elephants and Mountains* by Vivienne de Watteville

SELECTING QUESTIONS

Examiners spend a great deal of time choosing appropriate texts, setting questions, trialling them with students in schools, debating whether texts and questions are good enough.

Look at some sample questions below. The questions in each group aim to find similar answers, but they have slightly different wording. Discuss the strengths and weaknesses of the questions for each group, deciding which you would select for a real test paper. Copy the grid below and fill it in for question group 1, question group 2, etc.

Question group 1

a) What impression do you get of the narrator?
b) What is the narrator like?
c) Write down two words that sum up the narrator.
d) Which of these words best describe the narrator: brave, enthusiastic, interesting, adventurous, fearful, apprehensive, worried, foolhardy?

Question group 2

a) The writer says: 'I ran and ran as I have never run in my life before'. Why do you think she repeats the word 'ran' rather than just saying 'I ran as I have never run in my life before'?
b) Look at the writer's use of language in this sentence: 'I ran and ran as I have never run in my life before'. Why do you think the writer repeats the verb 'ran'?
c) The writer says: 'I ran and ran as I have never run in my life before'. What is the effect of the repetition of 'ran'?

Question group 3

a) How does the writer make the event with the rhino seem exciting?
b) How does the writer build tension in this extract?
c) How does the writer use words, phrases and sentences to make the scene dramatic?
d) How dramatic do you find the scene?

What are the questions aiming to find out?	
Which of the sample questions do you think works best? Why?	
Are there any further modifications you would make to your chosen question?	
What would you expect a really good answer to include?	

REMEMBER

Top candidates:
- ✦ judge the length and depth of their answer according to the number of points on offer
- ✦ embed brief quotations into their answers
- ✦ feel confident analysing language features.

SHAKESPEARE PAPER

The Shakespeare paper sets a question based on one of four broad topic areas:

 ✦ character and motivation
 ✦ ideas, themes, issues
 ✦ text in performance
 ✦ language of the text

Based on the scenes you are studying, look at the sample questions below. Then think up relevant questions that could be asked for your set scenes.

Theme	Sample question	Question on your chosen scenes
Character and motivation	✦ How does character X's personality seem different in the two extracts? ✦ How do the two extracts show that the character is unhappy about his recent decision?	
Ideas, themes and issues	✦ How do the extracts show the differences between women and men? ✦ How do the extracts show us that it is sometimes risky to jump to conclusions?	
Text in performance	✦ Imagine you were asked to direct these two extracts for a class performance. What advice would you give to actors playing the main parts? ✦ How should an actor show the changes of moods in character X?	
Language of the text	✦ What impression do you get of character X from the language she uses in these extracts? ✦ How does Shakespeare use language to build suspense in these two extracts? ✦ How does the language of character X show his changing moods?	

REMEMBER

Top candidates:
 ✦ know the extracts well
 ✦ build short quotations into their responses rather than have separate 'slabs' of quotations
 ✦ refer closely to the language.

WRITING PAPER

You will have two writing tasks – one longer (45 minutes allowed) and one shorter (30 minutes). Each task will address one of the 'writing triplets':

 ✦ Imagine, explore, entertain
 ✦ Inform, explain, describe
 ✦ Persuade, argue, advise
 ✦ Analyse, review, comment

Think about the text types you might be asked to write for each of these triplets. To start you off, think about which triplets each of these texts belongs to:

+ a leaflet aiming to ban boxing
+ the opening of a mystery story
+ a fact sheet for parents about school life
+ a speech about uniform
+ an account of a play you have just watched.

(LONGER WRITING TASK)

Main features:

+ the task carries 30 marks
+ you will have 45 minutes (including 15 minutes for planning)
+ the task is supported by information about audience, form, purpose and level of formality
+ a planning format is provided.

Look at the two sample tasks that follow.

Sample 1 You are the writer of detective books for children in which a school pupil, Alex Raven, solves mysteries. Write the opening of your new novel based on the newspaper article below.

Residents report 'night-time activity'

Local residents of the Priory Estate are expressing increasing concern about a pattern of night-time activity at the abandoned warehouse on West Road.

Their concerns include vans driving to and from the warehouse at night but never in daylight, and sounds of machinery from inside the building.

Pensioner Sue McGeever, 72, said "I don't sleep well at the best of times but all this activity is making my life a nightmare. I don't know what's going on, but the police need to act fast."

Notes for first chapter. Include:

+ ideas from this cutting for the storyline
+ description of atmosphere
+ lively dialogue

Planning frame
Notes on what might happen in this chapter
Character of Alex Raven
Notes for description and dialogue

Sample 2 Your tutor group has been asked to help promote healthy lifestyles in school. You have this note from the headteacher.

Health for Life

Everybody knows the importance of developing a healthy lifestyle. In school we want students to think carefully about what they eat and drink, and to take plenty of regular exercise.

If we are to make an impact, the healthy lifestyles message needs to come from students themselves rather than me.

Please let me have your proposal, in writing, for promoting a healthy lifestyle across the school.

Planning frame

My ideas for promoting a healthy lifestyle

How I will present these ideas to the headteacher

A persuasive opening for the proposal

1 When you have read the two sample tasks above, devise a fact sheet or poster to help other Year 9 students to do well on the tasks in test conditions. Work with a partner or in a small group.

Guide them on:
+ how to plan
+ how to make an impact at the start of their response
+ how to structure ideas clearly
+ how to use language in an interesting way.

Give them hints on how to use the planning frames and some examples of the style they might use in their responses.

2 Write part of a sample answer. Annotate it to show students what the strengths and weaknesses are of the response.

(SHORTER WRITING TASK)

Main features:
+ the task carries 20 marks, including 4 marks for spelling
+ you will have 30 minutes
+ the emphasis is on precision and cohesion
+ no planning format is provided but information about structure, audience and purpose is given.

First, read the two sample tasks that follow, then do the activities.

I Choose one of the writing tasks and, on your own or in a pair, write a really bad answer. Annotate it, showing why it is so bad. Under the text, list what the student needs to do to improve his or her answer.

Sample task 1

You have been wrongly accused of causing trouble in the school canteen. You have been sent to the Deputy Headteacher to explain yourself. Waiting outside the Deputy's office, you think about how you will prove your innocence.

You start to think about what you will say:

I know someone must have said they saw me when the argument in the canteen started, but it must be a mistake. I was in a rush today because of Drama Club, so …

Write the rest of your explanation.

Sample task 2

It is the start of the school year. You have been asked to talk to new students about how they can be most successful at school. You will be talking to them for five minutes in an assembly. Feeling nervous, you are determined to do a good job. You start like this:

Good morning everyone. I know just how you are feeling today. Starting at a new school is always nerve-racking. My job this morning is to give you some hints on how to make your life here as successful as possible, so here goes. First …

Continue the assembly talk, giving three main hints.

2 Read the list of language features below. Put them in rank order, starting with the one you think is most important for writing a good response to the shorter writing task.

- ✦ accurate spelling
- ✦ point of view (I, you or he/she/they)
- ✦ dialogue
- ✦ complex vocabulary
- ✦ accurate punctuation
- ✦ tense (past or present)
- ✦ description
- ✦ clear structure
- ✦ neat handwriting
- ✦ imaginative ideas

ASSESS YOUR LEARNING

Think carefully about what you need to do to improve your performance in the Key Stage 3 tests. Use the grid below to plan your preparation for the tests by identifying your strengths and weaknesses.

	Skills	Weak area	Sound	Strong area
Reading	Reading the booklet swiftly, but efficiently			
	Spotting key points in a text			
	Knowing what to say about a writer's style			
	Being able to comment on the writer's language			
	Using brief quotations			
Writing	Planning my answers			
	Getting the right style			
	Writing neatly enough			
	Structuring ideas into paragraphs			
	Using interesting techniques, e.g. different point of view/changing tense/using a split narrative			
	Choosing words that are precise and appropriate but neither predictable nor pretentious			
	Creating an effective overall structure			
	Working quickly enough			
	The requirements of the SHORTER writing task			
	The requirements of the LONGER writing task			
Shakespeare	Knowing my scenes in sufficient detail			
	Being clear what text in performance might involve			
	Knowing the key themes of the play			
	Being able to comment on the language of the scenes			
	Building short quotations into my answers			
	Structuring my response			